The Cancer Locker Room

Victor Mazzio

The Cancer Locker Room

Published by Mazzio Designs, LLC

December 2019

Copyright © 2019 by Victor Mazzio

All rights reserved.

Printed in the United States of America

First Printing, December 16, 2019

No part of this publication may be reproduced in any way or by any means without written permission from MAZZIO DESIGNS, LLC. Inquiries with regard to receiving written permission to reproduce any parts of this publication must be directed to MAZZIO DESIGNS, LLC.

ISBN 978-1-7343558-0-2

Names of all persons, institutions, businesses, and other entities of similar kind have been changed or omitted to protect those involved in this story.

All verses were written by Victor Mazzio and are the exclusive property of Victor Mazzio and MAZZIO DESIGNS, LLC.

Curious, quiet, and thoughtful to be,
Those things I would take from he.
A sense of earth .... a loving eye,
Those things I would take from she.

vfm

This book is dedicated to my parents and to my closest and best friend JMM. I thank them for holding safe the person that I am and the person that I am going to be.

My 3 children forever believe in me and encourage me in all things. I love them endlessly for giving me priority in their lives.

Early in my cancer journey, I chose heroes that mean the world to me. I knew these heroes would be the ones to carry me through all of the challenges that a cancer patient encounters. Thank you to these sacred few who have always been by my side with positive thoughts.

Prologue

Much like in sports, cancer patients have a 'locker room'. It has many spaces of existence. There are physical spaces such as hospital waiting rooms, oncology waiting rooms, medical specialist waiting rooms, medical testing waiting rooms, and treatment rooms. These physical spaces are where cancer patients often sit side by side and reflect on their life as a cancer patient. However, the real 'cancer locker room' resides in the hearts, souls, and minds of the patients who occupy the locker room—not in the physical spaces. This is true with sports locker rooms as well. The 'real locker room' is not the physical space that is occupied by the players. It is the space occupied by the singular mind, singular heart, and singular soul of the collective team of players.

People that are not on the team often think that the sacred locker room—where a team finds it's true identity—is the physical space that the players occupy. Sports reporters and other non-players may enter that physical 'sports locker room' space thinking that they are in the real locker room. While in that physical locker room space, they may also expect to uncover the real reasons for team success and team failure. These real reasons may never be uncovered because non-players almost never occupy the 'real locker room' space where player and team identities are formed and developed. Even though non-players may stand in the physical locker room space, they are almost never in the 'real locker room' as this is a space that is only ever reached by players on the team.

In parallel fashion, the same is true with cancer patients. There is a non-physical space involving the minds, hearts, and souls of cancer patients where one singular common identity forms and resides. This 'non-physical common identity' space for cancer patients is the 'cancer locker room'. This space has a peaceful beauty and purity about it. There is no competition in this space. There is no exclusion in this space. There is no judgement in this space. There is never any comparison in this space.

During breaks in treatment, the cancer patient gets to return to the reality of the world where competition, exclusion, judgement, and comparison exists. In the real world people have thoughts about who has the best house, who has the best car, who got the job promotion, and who looks the best. This real world 'achievement list' is endless. Real world 'achievement list' thinking is absent in the 'cancer locker room'—perhaps because everyone is placing great emphasis on the simple and essential things that sustain life. Getting to see another warm and brilliant sunshine. Getting to take another deep breath. Getting to smile, laugh, and cry knowing that all of those simple actions have profound meaning. In the 'cancer locker room', patients aren't interested in big cars, big houses, or having a cancer story worse than everyone else in the room. They never demean, discourage, or diminish others. Deep inside they inherently know that all of these things will not get them to the next day. Helping each other breath, smile, laugh, and cry gets them to the next day. Helping another find *hope* in an impossible situation gets them to the next day. God is present in the 'cancer locker room' and life in this room is the way God wants it to be.

I am excited for you to experience this book. I have tried my best to give you an idea of what life is like inside the 'cancer locker room'.

One

Two Stops on the 'T' and a Bus Ride to Hopkinton

So then one heart will make this plea,
Advance another sun to see,
To river past with still conceal,
Together walk persist appeal.

vfm

I kept a careful eye on the lump on my neck for roughly 4 months before I decided to see a doctor and have a biopsy. On a bright sunny day in September of 2010, I travelled to the office of my ENT doctor to get results of the needle biopsy that was done on the lump. I went into the office and before long I was in an examination room waiting to see the doctor. I could hear some arguing just outside of my examination room door. It sounded like the doctor was getting information from the nurse and the receptionist. Shortly after it became silent, my doctor entered the examination room and paused for a minute before giving me the news. "We just received results of the needle biopsy that we performed on the lump in your neck. You have a very advanced stage of Metastatic Melanoma. We will have blood tests, PET-CT, and MR imaging tests done to assign a more accurate stage to your cancer. It is likely that you have 5-6 months to live as we think the cancer is in a lymph node and we cannot locate a primary melanoma site. You may want to start speaking with hospice caregivers. Is there anyone that you would like for me to call? Will you need help getting home?"

There I sat in an examination room trying to figure out how I would get home to be with my wife. I needed for her to be near me—the fear was too big and too overwhelming. After the doctor gave me the news, he waited just a few minutes and for some reason thought that I should have some time to myself. He left the office. I felt like I couldn't move my legs but I only needed to get to my car so that I could get home. From running several marathons, I was thinking that the best way to get to the car would be to take one step at time …. think one thought at a time …. live one individual second at a time. My life changed dramatically in a 30-minute visit to a doctor's office. I would no longer be living in the 'weeks', 'months', and 'years'. I would now be doing the tedious work of living in the seconds'. Every day I would be living in the 'seconds'. Figuring out ways to get from one second to the next. Cancer moments are truly the loneliest moments that a person can experience. I just wanted people around me when I received the results of the biopsy and there I sat all alone. I realized in this short period of time that I would need a team of people to help me journey through cancer and conquer it.

Receiving a cancer diagnosis is usually the first step in a long, exhausting, and uncertain medical process. Sprinkled in with long periods of deep reflective thinking are distractions that give the mind a peaceful break. In this immediate moment, I was looking for something to think about that would take my mind away from thinking about the results of the biopsy. The marathons that I ran always gave me strength, hope, and a deeper understanding of who I am. I started to reflect on my past Boston Marathon experiences thinking that I might find strength for my long cancer journey …. a journey that would likely be the longest marathon of my life.

For self one act it is I do,
A bird to wing,
A star to shine.
Another thinks a thought to keep,
It could be this that I must seek.

vfm

So it is with a passion. Peace and balance created by that one thing that we do for ourselves and enjoy deeply. It warms the spirit, makes us a better person, and inspires others.

Six months in and four months out …. that's what some say about running marathons. If done right, it will take six months of high mileage training before the race and four months to get your mind and body back after the race. A rather large commitment and sacrifice by any measure. Especially if you lose—forever—a piece of yourself during the experience. If there is one worth doing it would be Boston. There is nothing quite like Patriot's day in April when the whole city of Boston takes a break to celebrate life …. and celebrate people pursuing their passion.

My first year there, I had it in mind to experience the

promise of Boston—deafening screams from students at Wellesley, challenging hills in Newton, and the exciting finish down Boyleston Street. After all, these are the things that get you through a marathon sometimes …. sensory distractions. Just like raising the volume on a radio to drown out the relentless appeals of life. Passing quickly and unknowingly from one unsavory moment to the next. Checking items off a list. Ultimately, responding to what is playing on the radio and not to the reality that is playing in the background. An acceptable way to get through a marathon but not the way I would get through this marathon. Someone had a different plan for me …. at a moment when I couldn't fill the air with distractions. I had to listen to what was playing in my life.

Race Day / 7:55am …. I jumped on the 'T' for two stops and then boarded a shuttle bus to Hopkinton where the race begins. An hour later we were in the 'Athletes Village' …. three hours until the start. Thousands of racers were milling around in an area the size of a football field on a cool New England morning. Each judging the fitness of the other by a race number displayed on a yellow plastic equipment bag—standard issue of the BAA (Boston Athletic Association). Low race numbers and good starting spots for those with fast qualifying times. High numbers and places nearer to the back of the 'pack' for those with slower qualifying times. Position earned— not negotiated or inherited. No loopholes for the unqualified. True and pure democracy at work.

Race Day / 9:15am .... I picked a spot on the grass about 30 yards from the main stage where a band was playing. A little too early to eat so I laid down and crumpled myself into a yoga posture. Nothing too extreme—just a simple stretch and some controlled breathing to turn my thoughts inward and get some focus. This would be a good day. I could feel things loosening up nicely.

Race Day / 9:35am .... Nervous energy got the best of me. I grabbed my race bag and went in search of the 'port-o-john' with the shortest line. Even though the full perimeter of the 'village' was occupied by them, the best I could do was a 20-minute wait. It was quite obvious that my planning and timing for future 'port-o-john' visits would have to improve if I was going to get to the starting line on time.

Race Day / 10:03am .... The number of racers increased with each passing minute. By now, there were about 9,000 of the 15,000 that would start the race. I managed to secure another spot on the grass and decided that this was a good time to have breakfast. A bagel, an apple, and a few handfuls of jelly beans—standard fare for most of my marathon adventures.

Race Day / 10:20am .... My wife and kids are just getting out of bed back at the hotel. Between 12 noon and one o'clock they will meet up with our cousin Andy somewhere close to the finish line on Boyleston. From there they plan to get updates on the computer as to where I will be on the course. A 'chip' transponder attached to my shoe will feed this information to the BAA data system at each 5K segment of the race. Projected finish time information will make it easy for them to wander and tour until I get close to finishing.

Race Day / 10:30am .... I thoroughly enjoy watching people cycle through the routines of the day. Reading a newspaper, drinking a cup of coffee, or securing their space and personalizing it. It tells so much about who they are and where they have been. Some are in constant motion …. others move very little. Some talk and interact continuously …. others find peace in solitude. Are those in constant motion 'chasing after the road' as in a short race? Are they seizing every opportunity and making the most of life? How about those who move at a slower pace? By 'letting the road come to them'—as in a marathon—are they missing out on some of the exciting things in this world that pass quickly through our grasp? Is their life less meaningf …. **"Do you mind if I sit here?"** came the question from above me. I panned up and my eyes fixed on the yellow bag that stood before me. Race number 6475. An older man …. probably got to Boston with a qualifying time between 3:25 and 3:30. **"Not at all"**, I replied. He pulled the bag from his shoulder and I gathered up my things to make room for him to sit. He introduced himself as Terry and told me that this would be his sixth Boston marathon.

Marathoners get to the start of their race with the help of many people. Some of it solicited and some in the form of unexpected gifts. For the racer, no distinction is ever made between the two. Both have equal importance when the goal is simply to start a 26-mile race. As the race unfolds, the person inside the racer feels something completely different. The gifts are very special. The gifts get your mind around the pain and carry you safely home.

My first serious attempt at qualifying for Boston 2001 came in November 2000 at the Philadelphia Marathon. My wife, children, and other family members came to cheer me to the finish. In some ways, I think they wanted Boston for me more than I wanted it for myself. On that day in Philadelphia, they made my life and my passion their priority. A special gift that I reflected upon often throughout the race. As it turned out, I would not reach Boston on that day. My second attempt would come at the Myrtle Beach Marathon in February.

Windy 60-degree air pressed against my face as I turned onto Kings Highway—just 10 miles into the race ....

typical conditions for Myrtle Beach in the middle of winter. Pete and Lee introduced themselves to me at mile 11. We were all running about the same pace so we decided to stay together for a while—at least until mile 20. At mile seventeen, we passed by my aunt's beach house on Ocean Boulevard. She was there cheering with my mother and my younger brother. So uplifting to see their warm smiles and hear their encouraging voices. I cried inside for my aunt. She was beginning a long journey of her own …. a battle with Parkinson's disease. The four of us made the 10-hour drive from Philadelphia just 2 days before this moment. I learned a lot about the three of them on the trip …. even more about myself. Two hours ago they gathered me in their arms—in my aunt's kitchen—praying that this would be my day. They along with Pete and Lee were my special gifts at Myrtle Beach.

Trouble came at mile 21 …. dizzy spells …. low energy …. a strong desire to quit. Deep within I could feel the work of my special gifts. There would be a way out of this. Pete and Lee looked strong so I encouraged them to continue on their way. All I needed was two or three miles at a slower pace to find the pieces that I lost and reassemble myself. Some sense of clarity and balance returned at mile 24. I passed by Pete who—in three short miles—was showing signs of complete delirium. His wife was on a bicycle next to him with fluids, encouragement, and the navigational pieces that he needed to get home. I was in a similar situation at the Buffalo Marathon in 1995. I remember that while this moment looked bad, the worst part of his struggle would come during the next several months of recovery. That is where the greatest demands on mental strength would be felt. Lee finished very strong in 3:06, I finished in 3:09, and Pete finished in 3:18. Lee and I would be going to Boston. Pete was just glad to finish and planned to take a full year of recovery before running another marathon.

Traveled oft a path is worn,
The river lost now finds a way.
A friend presents,
To news reveal,
Account of thoughts,
With heart to feel.

vfm

Terry is a college professor from Colorado. His wife and son Zach accompanied him on the five previous Boston Marathons that he ran. He was doing this one alone because his wife and Zach needed to be in Chicago with family. It seemed fine for Terry to spend a few days in Boston for the marathon.

During our time in the 'village', Terry and I talked about

all the things that casual acquaintances never get around to discussing. Thoughtful topics explored by only the closest of friends. Marriage, children, and finding the strength to actively practice family values that we all know are important. We both agreed that a return and firm commitment to these values could raise our troubled youth above the violence that they create—an unsettling sort of violence that is becoming more savage, spiteful, and frequent. All of us are a part of this fascinating 'social puzzle' and should be made to feel so …. each minute of every day.

My wife and children bought me a 2001 Boston Marathon jacket. Terry got one also. To me it's the kind of jacket that gets very little wear. Almost like a special trophy for participating in the marathon. Mine would rest in the closet and get pulled out every now and then when my heart needed a reminder and my spirit needed a lift. Terry bought his jacket for Zach who developed a special love for the sport and a special love for his father. Watching his father is always more than enough. Doctors in Chicago were working to make Zach feel more comfortable with the affliction that silenced his legs many years ago but he will never be able to run with his father. Zach is eternally hopeful and follows a father who chases after a passion that brings new days with bright, warm sunshine. The special gift of Zach brought Terry to this 'village' for a sixth Boston. The ability to inspire and excite a 'close heart' would carry him to the finish. Terry was running for the both of them.

It seems that practicing a passion creates an awareness or sensibility for things that are normally missed. Others are inspired to be part of the excitement that we show. In the process, there is a real possibility of getting to know the pieces of our 'self' that reside in the hidden corners of our conscience. Life becomes a breathtaking and endless journey to retrieve these pieces. Contextual interaction with others brings pieces of who we are to the surface of our thinking. To understand more deeply, we turn around these pieces in our mind. The puzzle of who we are and how we fit in this world takes shape on a daily basis.

Within this smile one fear to live,
On subtle step does life persist.
Take of this hand for guide belong,
Till tear release with moment gone.

vfm

Terry introduced me to the 'real' gift of the Boston Marathon. He helped me to see the gift that comes from practicing a passion. All of it is right there in the 'Athletes Village' at Hopkinton. Qualifying for Boston is the key that opens the lock on 15,000 stories of struggle and expression of human spirit. Individuals come to Boston representing the efforts and hopes of many. Terry taught me that the pieces of our individual spirit lay sprinkled in the hearts and minds of those who surround us. The task at our feet is to create situations where we exchange with others—offering up the piece of their identity that we hold and retrieving the piece of our identity that they hold.

After about 20 minutes, the doctor came back into the examination room and started to describe the tests that would be done over the next several weeks. At the end of testing, I was scheduled to see an oncologist to discuss a treatment plan. I was able to make my way out of the doctor's office but needed to run to my car as it had just started to rain. I made the short drive home and was finally with my wife.

I told my wife everything through the tears in my eyes and the pain in my throat. I tried to be strong for her but the stronger I tried to be, the more I broke down. She was quiet the whole time just trying to process what she was hearing. The news of my cancer shocked both of us.

Just a few days after receiving the biopsy results, I was in the hospital for bloodwork. There was nothing unique about the bloodwork that was done. As I waited to have my blood drawn, I noticed that others in the waiting room were normal everyday patients. In my hopeful mind I was feeling like I might have been misdiagnosed. Nothing about this testing made me feel like I had just 5-6 months to live.

A couple of days after bloodwork, I went back to the hospital for a full body MRI both with and without contrast. This is where my condition became very real for me. I noticed that there were many cancer patients in the waiting room. Some of these cancer patients were in wheelchairs and seemed to be residents in the hospital. Others appeared to be having scans done as outpatients like me. Still others must have been in the middle of cancer treatments as they looked very sick and very exhausted—many in this group were slumped over in their wheelchairs and appeared to be unresponsive to the questions they were being asked and the conversations that surrounded them. Many of those waiting for MR Imaging and PET/CT imaging had very little hair and a greyish complexion. I didn't belong here. I was not as sick as all of these people.

I sat next to Michael for the short 15 minutes that I spent in the MR imaging waiting room. Michael was 32 years old and in his words had "an amazing wife 'Mags' and 2 beautiful daughters—Emily and Cara". He cried when he told me that Emily—his 4 year old daughter—wondered who he was going to visit when he left for cancer treatments each week for 4 days. She loved her father's 'new bald head' and missed reading stories and having tea parties in the mornings on the days when he was not home. Cara—his 2 year old daughter—wanted to do everything that Emily was doing and loved her father dearly. She was part of the morning tea parties and missed having them with her father just as much as Emily did. Michael showed me a picture where he was escorting the girls into their morning tea party. Mags took the picture. Michael admitted that tea parties with his girls made leaving for treatments hard but returning home from treatments easy. He loved the tea parties because he knew that when he was at a tea party with his girls, he was still alive …. the cancer hadn't yet beaten him. Mags started the tea parties as a way for him to be with the girls. She wanted Michael to have moments with his daughters that every father usually has when daughters get into their teens and twenties. Moments like "Father-Daughter" dances and weddings. Mags made this a special time for just the girls and Michael. He said that Mags was so afraid to lose him that she wanted this special time for the three of them.

Beside this tree,
My rest for thee,
For of one heart,
Our souls to be.

vfm

Michael loved Mags for this gift and he told her almost every day. He had cancer in his right kidney and lungs. So far the treatments didn't diminish his cancer but he believed in his doctors and would be forever hopeful.

The MR imaging chamber is a small confined space so I thought I might feel claustrophobic during the test. The night before my imaging, I deprived myself of sleep thinking that I could close my eyes and sleep while my scans were being recorded. This plan worked perfectly for me. I was placed in the MR imager and for 25 minutes a full body scan was captured. I was moved in and out of the chamber without feeling a thing and without seeing a thing. Even with earplugs inserted in my ears, I could hear an occasional loud bang or series of bangs from the instrument as it followed an orchestrated set of duties.

After 25 minutes of background scanning without a

contrast agent in my body, I was injected with a solution that contained glucose—each glucose molecule containing a magnetically active gadolinium atom. Cancer sites love sugar (glucose) so the injected glucose solution tends to preferentially concentrate at cancer sites that may exist in the body. In this way, an enhanced magnetic response in the MR instrument—from the gadolinium atom present in each glucose molecule—is recorded at cancer sites within the body …. ultimately giving pictures of body sites where cancer exists.

I felt a cool sensation immediately after the gadolinium contrast solution was injected into my arm. The nurse let me rest for a few minutes before MR scans 'with contrast' were recorded. I closed my eyes again and was able to fall partially asleep as the instrument table moved me into and out of the large magnet. After 25 minutes of scanning 'with contrast', I was moved out of the large magnet and was able to sit up on the instrument table as I put on my belt, shoes, and watch. I could see into the glass enclosure where the nurse was and I noticed that several doctors were in the room with her. They were pointing to a computer monitor where they were probably looking at the MR images that were recorded on my body. Every once in a while they would look out at me before looking back at the computer monitor. This really scared me as I could only think that they were seeing lots of cancer in the images. After about 10 minutes, the doctors left and the nurse came back into the MR imaging room. She showed me how to get back out to the waiting room and choked on a few of her words as she let me know that my oncologist would be discussing the test results with me in about a week.

Two days after my MR image testing, I came back to the same area of the hospital for full body PET/CT images. As with the MR imaging, I was scheduled to have PET/CT images recorded 'with contrast'. Being a chemist, I knew going into the scans that the contrast agent for my images would be a radioactive fluorine isotope attached again to a glucose type molecule. Just like with MR imaging, a type of glucose 'carrier' molecule is used since this molecule has a preferential affinity for cancer sites in the body. Cancer just loves glucose and brilliant researchers use it to understand the size and spatial position of cancer sites in our bodies. I also knew going in that the CT part of the total scan is essentially used to give an outline of bone structure in the body which is ultimately used to accurately register body features—heart, lungs, kidneys, etc.—and cancer sites that are detected by the PET part of the scan.

I was brought into a 'prep' room where I was to be injected with the FDG contrast agent through a needle syringe that was covered by a stainless steel cylinder. This stainless steel shield protected the nurse from radiation exposure as she made the injection. There were two reclining lounge chairs in the prep room. I was in one of them and Frank was in the other. He was in his chair when I first entered the room but we were both injected at about the same time. We were each told that we would wait 30-45 minutes for the contrast agent to move through our body. While we waited, we had to drink about 32 ounces of a barium solution that would help the imaging of our esophagus and stomach. Frank and I called this drink our 'radioactive cocktail'. We sat together enjoying our medical milkshakes as we caught up on the cancer roads that we were traveling.

Frank was like a father to me. He was free of cancer for 6 years and the cancer had returned. His right ear was taken by his cancer and his hearing was taken in that ear as well. He told me to speak to his left ear and it worked perfectly for all that he wanted to know about me. He was concerned about my cancer and how I was getting along. I told him that I was a little over a week into my journey. I let him know that I was more afraid than I have ever been in my life. My wife and 3 children really needed me. We were much too early in our lives together and I felt like our story was just beginning. My cancer was a fight that I could not lose.

Frank was a widower and a grandfather to 3 beautiful children—one little boy and two little girls. His daughter was heartbroken to learn that his cancer had returned. She wanted him around for her children because they all loved the times that they spent with 'Gramps.' Frank seemed like a simple guy with a big heart. He taught the children how to care for his dog 'Peanut' and how to understand what a dog is really all about. He taught me that laughter was important at times like this and positive thinking was even more important. He let me know that I would likely encounter people during my cancer journey—people not in the 'cancer locker room'—that would doubt that I even had cancer and doubt with an even stronger will that I wasn't even going to a hospital or cancer center for cancer treatment. "These are the ones that must be ignored. They will never understand the most important parts of our cancer walks—the parts that are hard to put into words but are intuitively known by fellow cancer patients. You and I will know the true cancer story and the true struggles about each other before the story is ever told. Without any doubting, our most positive thoughts will come from those who love us the most and from those who suffer from cancer like us." Before we parted ways and went to our separate rooms for scanning, he told me that I would become strong and begin to heal as soon as I put my whole life into the hands of the doctors and nurses that I trust the most. In his words he said, "go out and find that group of doctors, nurses, family, and friends that you trust the most and push all of your chips to the center of the table on them." This was the best advice of all.

Shattered thoughts,
One reach away,
On weep to friend,
Of heart to stay.

vfm

I think about Frank all the time. I pray that he still takes long walks with 'Peanut', his daughter, and his grandchildren …. always hearing the best from the people that he passes along the way.

My first round of testing was finished. I was on my way to see an oncologist that was recommended to me by the ENT doctor that first gave me the news of my cancer …. just two short weeks ago. I entered the oncologist's office along with my wife and we took a seat in the waiting room. Before long we were taken to an examination room and left to wait a bit longer for the oncologist. Her office was next to our examination room and while we waited we could hear—through the wall that separated us—a conversation that she must have been having on her phone because she was the only one that we could hear. It was a loud conversation so we didn't have to listen intently to hear the words that she was speaking. She was giving details about my cancer biopsy, my bloodwork, the MRI, and the PET/CT tests that were done. She was certainly having a conversation with someone about my cancer condition. As the conversation went on, we sat there wondering …. Who was she speaking to? Who was on the other end of the conversation? The conversation got really loud at points and we heard her say, "There must be something that we can do! …. There has to be a treatment that will work for the metastatic melanoma condition that he has!" She continued, "Well I am about to meet with him and his wife and I can't tell him that we do not have a definitive treatment for him! What do you think I should tell him?" At this point, my wife and I were silent. I didn't know what to think. Coming into this appointment with my oncologist, I thought that there was always some treatment to try with cancer. There are clinical trials and—at the very least—there are 'low chance of success' therapies. From the way a cancer patient thinks, there are never any 'completely hopeless' situations. Maybe I watched too many cancer movies where you are led to think that every cancer patient is undergoing some kind of treatment. Maybe my metastatic melanoma cancer condition was really a 'no available therapy' situation. This was sounding like a replay of my biopsy news of two weeks ago. I was frozen in my seat. I wasn't going to just give up and accept a grace-filled and pity-filled exit from this world. At this very moment, I heard—through the wall—my oncologist say the full name of the person that she was speaking to on the phone. It ended up being a very important doctor at a nearby 'premier' cancer institute. We no longer heard my oncologist speaking loudly in the other room. Perhaps her conversation was finished. Minutes after we heard silence in the adjoining room, the door to my examination room opened. My oncologist stood in the doorway, silently looking across the room at me and my wife. It looked like she had been crying. She took one step into our room and started to cry. She was holding my cancer folder in her hands. The pink folder in her hands had several tiny faded spots sprinkled on it from where her tears had fallen. I felt so bad that she had to go through the challenges that she faced with my cancer.

She walked quickly across the room and placed the one remaining chair in the room next to mine. As she started to sit, she took my left hand into her right hand and took my wife's right hand into her left hand. We were sitting in a close circle holding hands as she revealed that my cancer was stage 4 metastatic melanoma and that it was primarily located in a lymph node in the back of my neck. She went on to say that the tumor growth in that lymph node was roughly the size of a golf ball—in terms of the volume that it occupied. PET/CT testing also showed regions of high FDG uptake in several nodular spots within both of my lungs. In translation, this meant that there were cancerous nodules in both of my lungs as well. She indicated that the stage 4 classification of my cancer came from the lack of knowing the whereabouts of a primary melanoma site on my skin or elsewhere, the fact that my cancer growth was in a lymph node, and the fact that I had cancerous nodules in both of my lungs. She shared all of this information with both me and my wife through the tears in her eyes. What a very sad time for all three of us. I think we all felt hopeless and defeated.

She started to talk about a treatment plan for my cancer and sadly revealed that there were really no therapies currently available that could be used to fight my cancer. The lump on my neck could be surgically removed but beyond that there was not much that could be done. She went on to say that if I wished, I could have interferon treatments after the surgery to boost my immune system and possibly extend my life for about a year. If I decided to receive interferon treatments after surgery, she said that I would probably have 'flu-like' symptoms the entire time that I was receiving the treatment.

I learned that doctors become very human in moments like these. When she was finished sharing this news with me and my wife, she completely broke down in tears and said that she was very sorry for not being able to provide a therapy for my cancer. I immediately told her that we needed to be strong and positive. Somehow we would get through this little 'bump' in my road.

On the day that we received this news, I could not have made it home from the oncologist's office without my wife by my side. Together we left her office knowing that we needed to make a difficult and thoughtful decision as to who we would have perform the surgery to remove the cancer tumor from my neck. Even more difficult would be the conversation that we now needed to have with our 3 children—letting them know that I have cancer.

Two

Town!

First step with guide from step of past,
A second feels the breeze direct,
Of two a one will walk through change,
To shake this branch and bring along.

vfm

'Big Meet' Saturday for the high school varsity girls' cross country team that I coached. The day before the race, we walked the course then sat for a bit discussing what our race strategies would be. Before too long, I read to them a motivational letter that I wrote—hoping that it would get them 'charged up' for our big race the next day.

"Cross Country Girls,

A few weeks ago, we sat together and had one of our 'heart-to-heart' conversations. It didn't start out as a 'heart-to-heart' but it soon elevated to that level.

Mari shared her hopes for herself and for the team in a way that brought many of us to tears. For me it was all good because I felt refreshed and invigorated—not drained. Thanks Mari for showing us a piece of your heart.

During our conversation, I talked about my hopes for the team and admitted that I had a personal reason for coming to be your coach—a reason which you would someday come to know. I guess it didn't seem like the right moment for me to share THAT piece of my heart.

I feel like we have grown our friendships since then so I have picked this race dedication to let you know my personal reason for being with you each afternoon as your cross country coach.

The reason begins with my parents. They don't do anything earth shattering—they just love me. By some measures it isn't enough for a parent to just love a child. For me it has been everything because they have expressed it in a way that has made me feel like I am the centerpiece in their lives. Their mark on me is indelible …. and I have let it be so. I always hear their voice and feel their presence—wherever I go.

I remember once when I was about 10 years old. Me, my brothers, and some friends contrived the perfect plan for playing soccer at night. We decided that instead of a lighted soccer field, we would set the ball on fire and play in the dark. Conceptually, this seemed perfect. We took a tennis ball, soaked it in lighter fluid, lit it, and headed out to the asphalt street for our first game. What we didn't know was that the street had just been paved and it still contained flammable solvents. Unfortunately, we had created one of the largest bonfires that I had ever seen. This fire stood about 10 feet high and burned over one block of asphalt roadway. The fire extinguished itself very quickly and luckily no damage to the road was done. Needless to say, that was the first time that I really heard my father's voice and really felt his presence. I'm almost certain that this is when I first became interested in running. It was probably my very first 'interval speed workout'.

I have experienced many things since the mistakes that I made in my younger days, but none has been harder for me to deal with than the death of my father late last year. He struggled for 13 years with Alzheimer's before giving in at the age of 67. My mother cared for him the whole way.

He stayed in nursing homes and each day my mother would wash his clothes, feed him, and pray with him. Her strength throughout his illness gave all of us the strength and the time to say goodbye. I was particularly saddened by the idea that he would never get to celebrate the good things that his children were doing. He got to hold our daughter once—when she was about 4 months old—before he no longer knew who she was. I think we all lost a piece of ourselves as we watched the disease change him from a dignified 167 pound person to a quiet and withdrawn 72 pound saint. I know that he would be proud of the time that I am spending here with you. He would certainly be impressed with you as people and the things that you accomplish as runners.

One of the lessons that my father taught me was that good people bring about positive change. He would see—as I have—that all of you have the potential and opportunity to take the world in new directions. He would also see—as I have—that you are good people. This is my sole reason for coming to be your coach. I BELIEVE IN THE PROMISE OF YOUR POTENTIAL. I also believe that you will come to appreciate how the struggles of running—just as the struggles of life—make the articulation of that potential more real. I encourage you to think through the struggles that you face in running. Don't simply dismiss them or bury them. A deeper understanding of these struggles leads to a deeper understanding of yourself. As you work through these challenges, be receptive to the thoughts of those who know you well. My parents have always been—and remain—noble custodians of my identity. For the commitment they have made to the health of my spirit, I would like to dedicate this race to them.

I was telling you during our 'heart-to-heart' that I cry at some movies and I mentioned 'October Sky' as one of those movies. The final scene in the movie reminds me of the times that I will never have with my father. In that scene, Homer Hickam—one of the 'Rocket Boys'—is about to launch his final rocket. His father shows up for the launch—after missing all of the previous launches—and puts his arm around Homer while they watch the rocket soar into the sky. For me, the rocket represents the people and things in my life that my father would be proud to know—my children, my wife, my career, and you. I get upset when I realize that he will never be by my side to watch my 'rockets' soar.

As the final part of this race dedication, I have a wish for each of you. It is best expressed in the following verse ….

That your parents always be by your side,
Their arms on your shoulders,
Their eyes fixed above,
Looking on with pride and fascination,
As your 'rockets' climb through the sky,
To a place that all in the world can see.

vfm

Thank you for allowing me to make this race dedication. It has a very special meaning in my life.

Run hard.

Let your heart lead you home."

Hearts release in unison trigger,
Song be told of youths' deliver.
Print upon a path made shallow,
Giving life to earth once fallow.

vfm

One year after this amazing year of running for the cross country girls, I had family obligations and growing obligations at my work that took up all of my time. I left the program and many members on the girls' and boys' track and cross country teams felt like they wanted to thank me for the time I spent with them each day …. teaching them how to run farther and faster than they ever thought they could. They sent me hand written notes and emails but the most surprising and uplifting 'thank you' that they gave to me were nominations to be a torchbearer for the Salt Lake 2002 Olympic Torch Relay. Emails with the following text were flooding into my email inbox. Many from athletes on the team but also an astronomical number of emails from people that I didn't even know. Somehow the 'word' to nominate me to be a torchbearer got around. This nomination was submitted by Emily ….

"You've been nominated to be a torchbearer in the Salt

Lake 2002 Olympic Torch Relay. Emily has nominated you to help carry the Olympic Flame in the 2002 Olympic Torch Relay, presented by Coca-Cola and Chevrolet. Did you know the passing of the Olympic Flame dates back to the first Olympic Games held in ancient Greece? Now, you have a chance to be a part of that tradition by participating in this exciting event.

Here's the Torch Relay lowdown.

The Torch Relay kicks-off on December 4th 2001 and will travel through 46 states before hitting Salt Lake City, Utah, home of the 2002 Olympic Winter Games. Coke is looking for torchbearers who have demonstrated courage, dedication, inspiration, passion and/or a caring and giving spirit.

Coke has already chosen Lance Armstrong to carry the Olympic Flame for part of its' journey. If you're selected to join him as a torchbearer, you'll get all the details in the mail."

I was never selected to be part of the 2002 Olympic Torch Relay but I learned a lot about the value and importance of 'teams' and the strength of unity from that famed girls' cross country team.

Teamwork is so essential to achieving impossible things. Even the most impactful individual achievements are realized through team efforts. I witnessed this with the girls' cross country team, with the baseball teams that I coached, and with the team sports that I played—both in high school and in college. I was thinking that beating cancer would be no different. In order to reach remission and have my body and mind be completely free of cancer, I would need a team of people that were close to me …. a team of people that had an enduring concern for my life. This group would take up the 'fight' during times when I was discouraged or low on energy. At times, this group would want more for me than I would want for myself.

Shortly after our first meeting with the oncologist, I started to share parts of my cancer story with others and my team seemed to be forming naturally. There was no formal process. It all started when my wife and I shared the news of my cancer with our 3 children.

We gathered at a nearby pizza kitchen to talk about my cancer. There were a lot of questions but not a lot of answers. I was given just enough information by my doctors and the tests that were done to paint a rather gloomy picture for our children. I didn't tell them that my cancer was stage 4. I didn't tell them that the doctors seemed desperate and hopeless about my situation. I didn't tell them that some of the doctors were talking about hospice care and 5-6 months to live. I wanted them to know enough to remain hopeful and to become my 'heroes'—that very close group of people that would give me a forever look of confidence and assurance, especially when I needed it. So I spoke to them through the hope and the strength that I had developed over the last three weeks of being surprised and saddened by the doctors and the tests that were done. One thought that stuck with me was expressed by my daughter—our oldest child. She wasn't yet engaged to be married but she asked me, "Will you be there for my wedding when I get married?" I assured her that I would be there and that I would be so happy when I walked her down the aisle. In my heart, I was really concerned about whether or not I would be around to walk her down the aisle.

I came away from our family gathering feeling like they loved me a ton. I felt like they could—and would—take my hand and lead me when I lost my way in this cancer journey. When I was about 14, I remember my father saying to me that I needed to learn how to speak the words that often got trapped inside of my head. He told me that people need to be a part of that 'inner conversation' that always seems to be running inside of me—especially those that are close to me. On that special day—when we made the children a part of my cancer journey—I let them be a part of my 'inner conversation'. I showed them genuine vulnerability just like my doctors showed me genuine vulnerability and they reacted to me with love and confidence. Surely it was sad news, but I think we grew very close as a family on that day.

After the conversations that I had with my ENT 'biopsy' doctor and my current oncologist, I decided that I needed to be in the hands of a group of doctors that weren't frightened by my stage 4 metastatic melanoma cancer situation. I needed to be around doctors that see patients like me all the time and aren't discouraged by patients with a cancer condition like mine. I didn't need to be part of hopeless conversations. Positive thoughts got my mind to this point so I began to think of how I could become a patient of doctors at a nearby 'premier' cancer institute where ground breaking work was being done with melanoma.

After perusing the scientific publications of oncologists who were doing research leading to clinical trials at this 'premier' cancer institute, I noticed that there were two researchers in particular that were doing very progressive work in the area of melanoma. One of them had recently left to further some parts of their collaborative work in New England while the other stayed behind to continue working with melanoma patients at the 'premier' cancer institute. I was intent on getting an appointment with this oncologist that decided not to leave.

After gathering together all of my test results from both my ENT 'biopsy' doctor and my current oncologist, I repeatedly called the office of this remaining expert melanoma oncologist at the 'premier' cancer institute and was not able to connect with anyone in his office. The next day I took all of my test results to the 'premier' cancer institute and sat in the atrium of their cancer center for the entire morning trying to speak with anybody in his office by phone. By 1pm in the afternoon, I finally connected with a receptionist in his office and learned that he was still taking melanoma cancer patients as long as surgeries were not yet performed and treatments had not yet been started. I satisfied both of these criteria so I was able to schedule an appointment to see him in three weeks. What a stressful time this was for me but I was committed in my heart to having the best chance of beating my cancer. I felt confident that with this particular oncologist, I would have the best chance of winning my cancer battle.

I entered the office of my new oncologist—at the nearby 'premier' cancer institute—and checked in with the receptionist. She collected my previous test results and told me and my wife to take a seat in the waiting room. After about a 20-minute wait, we were back in an examination room—one step closer to seeing the oncologist that I had been waiting to see for 3 long weeks.

He had time to look through the results of my blood tests, MRI scans, my PET/CT scans, and my biopsy before he entered our examination room …. and he did so very thoroughly. He entered the room, introduced himself, and immediately began discussing my cancer. It was obvious that he had done a thorough review of the initial set of tests that were done on me. My sister-in-law worked as a nurse at the 'premier' cancer institute. She joined me and my wife at this first appointment with my new oncologist.

Not once during our appointment did he make predictions or share thoughts about how long I had to live. He made very clear statements about what we needed to do and how we would step our way through his treatment plan. He also recommended that I not read 'blogs'—or literature of any kind—on survival statistics or treatment plans for melanoma cancer patients. His logic for making this recommendation was very simple. We would be using the best and most 'up-to-date' technology available to beat my cancer. Every cancer journey is unique and different so we didn't need to be distracted by treatment plans that didn't fully apply to my cancer. In the last half of my appointment, we discussed my neck surgery and his ideas on who he thought should perform the surgery. He recommended one of the best head and neck surgeons in the country who was currently the head of the otorhinolaryngology department at the 'premier' cancer institute. I had spoken to some close friends who had similar surgeries—on benign neck tumors—that were performed by another surgeon in the same department. This 'other' surgeon was also world renowned in the field of head and neck surgery. I expressed my preference for him and my oncologist agreed wholeheartedly with my choice. My oncologist arranged to have me meet with this surgeon in about a week so that he could examine me, review my records, and schedule my surgery. My oncologist also scheduled an immediate appointment for a full eye examination with an eye specialist and an immediate appointment with a dermatologist. After I had my first appointment with the dermatologist, my oncologist instructed me to see the dermatologist on a regular basis so that he could detect any melanomas that appear on my skin or perhaps detect a possible re-appearance of a 'primary site' for the melanoma that was in my neck lymph node.

I met with the eye specialist and went through testing for 2 hours. He had spoken with my new oncologist and understood my cancer situation very well. He would be doing a complete examination of my eyes to learn if there were indications of melanoma in or around my eyes. I was curious as to why my oncologist ordered this study so I asked the eye specialist. He told me that melanoma develops in melanocyte cells and this cell type is located primarily in the skin, eyes, ears, and gastrointestinal areas of the body. He went on to say that with this knowledge of where melanocyte cells reside in the body, it makes sense to fully examine these areas of the body when melanoma is discovered—especially in a lymph node. He said that my metastatic melanoma was unique in that it was first detected in a lymph node which in most melanoma cases is a late stage condition. Most melanomas initially present—and are detected—at a 'primary site' on the skin, in the eyes, or in the gastrointestinal areas of the body. This 'primary melanoma site' will often 'broadcast' mutated melanocyte cells (melanoma) to other parts of the body as part of the melanoma propagation process.

The eye specialist looked into my eyes with illuminated optical microscope instruments and took pictures as he went. His assistants recorded a full set of images of my eyes as well. He developed a baseline of my current eye condition from all of the tests that he performed and from all of the images that he collected. Future eye tests and images would be compared against this baseline to reveal changes that may be related to a progression of my cancer. In one of his final tests, he examined my eyes specifically for the presence of melanoma. Even though he would report all of his findings to my oncologist—and I would eventually get to hear the findings from my oncologist at our next appointment, he was getting 'real time' information on whether or not melanoma was in or around my eyes. During this test he did not find melanoma anywhere in or around my eyes. Finally, I was getting good news about my condition. This was a great day.

Less than one day after eye testing, I visited with my dermatologist. He examined my skin thoroughly for signs of melanoma. As with the eye specialist, he formed a baseline of my current skin condition from his observations. Any future observations would be compared against this baseline to see if changes had occurred that possibly related to my current melanoma condition. During his examination he found some 'curious' sites which he biopsied. These sites were determined to be basal cell carcinoma and squamous cell carcinoma. He excised these sites just one week later on a return visit. I was scheduled to visit with him every three months for the next 2 years.

With grasp on spade,
To stand behind,
What earth shall give,
In moment find.

vfm

I had chosen a truly gifted head and neck surgeon. His abilities and his personality were perfect for me. I met with him on a rainy Tuesday. I made my way from the waiting room to an examination room—along the way seeing things that scared me and reminded me that I still didn't feel as sick as the patients that surrounded me.

While in the waiting room, I sat next to Barry before we both were taken to our examination rooms. Barry had a large 'gauze-like' covering over his entire nose. We sat quietly for quite some time—watching a fishing show that was playing on the television. Before long, he leaned over and asked me if I had ever been fishing. I told him that when I was about 9, I fished at a lake when we were on vacation in the mountains. This was the first time—and probably the only time—that I had ever fished. I told him that it seemed like a lot of waiting for—sometimes—no big reward. Things moved too slow for me when it came to fishing so I never really got interested in it. Barry told me that he and his Uncle Bill used to fish all the time. They fished out in the Chesapeake Bay on—what seemed like—one day out of every week during the year. Most of the time they would just release the fish because they wanted to get good at luring and catching fish. His Uncle Bill wanted to feel like he could 'out-think' the fish. Barry and his Uncle Bill spent years together catching fish. They would leave early in the morning and on most of the fishing trips they returned late in the evening. Barry grew up around his Uncle Bill. Barry's father died at a young age—when Barry was around 11 years old—so Uncle Bill treated Barry like a son and Barry saw his Uncle Bill as a father.

When Barry was around 21 years old, his Uncle Bill became very sick and they didn't get to fish very much anymore. Barry really missed this time that they used to have together on the boat. Everything about fishing was interesting to the both of them. Maintaining the boat, getting the boat ready for a day of fishing, making the lures, gathering up all of their fishing gear, and getting out on the water. Barry said that he tried going fishing by himself during Uncle Bill's illness but it wasn't the same. It really seemed like this was something that could be done only when him and his Uncle were on the boat. Just 5 months after Uncle Bill got sick, he passed away from cancer that started in his pancreas and ended up ravaging his entire body. Barry was a pallbearer at the funeral and was really sad to see his Uncle go.

Just before being called into an examination room, Barry said that he was suffering from cancer in his sinuses and up around his eyes. About three months ago he had surgery to remove the cancer and he was now being evaluated for reconstructive surgery on his nose. He just loved our surgeon and really looked forward to visiting with him each time that he came into the office.

Shortly after Barry went back into the examination room area, I was called by a nurse and asked to follow her back beyond the front office area. Along the way to my room, we passed by the examination room occupied by Barry. He had the 'gauze-like' covering off of his nose and he didn't have a nose at all. There was—what looked like—a hole in his head where his nose used to be. It was truly the most devastating thing that I have ever seen. He looked up as I passed by and we both smiled at each other. He had that forever optimistic smile on his face and I was so encouraged when I saw him for that one final time. This was truly one of the most uplifting moments while I was in the 'cancer locker room'—seeing someone that I got to know just a little bit, being so excited about every new day.

I sat down in my examination room chair and waited for my surgeon to come into the room. I brought my previous test results with me and gave them to the nurse as she asked me a bunch of medical questions. Each answer that I gave got entered into the medical profile that was gradually being built on me. The nurse left and closed the door behind her. After about 10 minutes, she returned with the doctor. He quickly reviewed the medical results that I gave to him and then began to examine my nose, sinuses, and throat for any indications of cancer. His examination lasted about 15-20 minutes, after which we began to discuss possible dates for my surgery. We were already into the middle of October—about 5 weeks after I had a first biopsy on the tumor in my neck. He opened up some surgery dates in his calendar for me in late November and in early December. He said that we could possibly wait until the first or second week in January but he really wanted to have the surgery done before Thanksgiving. For the sake of understanding, I asked him why he wanted to perform the surgery before Thanksgiving. He said that he felt my surgery should be done soon so that I would have time to rest and build back my health for other treatments that follow the surgery. My wife and I picked a surgery date in November—almost exactly two weeks before Thanksgiving. My surgeon also ordered a 'pre-surgery' MRI scan—both with and without contrast—on my head and neck. This scan was scheduled to be done 2 weeks before the surgery.

I returned to the 'premier' cancer institute for my MRI scans during the last week in October. It was a detailed set of head and neck MRI scans that would be recorded. I entered the imaging room and was inserted into the big MR magnet imaging tube with an RF coil surrounding my entire head. As with my first set of MR imaging scans, I closed my eyes and tried to reach a state of calm …. almost falling asleep as I was moved into and out of the imaging tube. After about 20 minutes, I was moved out of the magnet tube and injected with the gadolinium contrast solution. Ten minutes after injection, I was re-inserted into the instrument magnet tube with the RF head coil surrounding my entire head once again. Scanning was finished twenty minutes later and I was moved out of the imaging tube for good. I noticed all of the doctors and a few nurses gathered in the instrument control room behind a glass window. They were likely making sure the scans were acceptable for the purposes of my head and neck surgeon. I think they were being certain that the collected images showed accurate position and size information for my cancer tumor. A short while later, I was released from the imaging room and allowed to go home.

One week after MR imaging, I went to see my head and neck surgeon. He quickly reviewed the MR images with me showing me the size and position of the cancer tumor. It was clearly located in a lymph node and occupied a volume comparable to that of a golf ball. It measured a little over 5 centimeters on a 'long axis' and a little over 3 centimeters on a 'short axis'. A normal healthy lymph node is about the size of a pea. Amazingly, the lymph node in my neck that contained the tumor was enlarged by 40 times its' normal size in order to accommodate the metastatic melanoma tumor. My surgeon was amazed and concerned that this was the case. He was prepared to learn that the tumor may be in more than one lymph node when he exposed the cancer site during surgery. The surgery was classified as a 'right neck dissection'. If all went as planned, I would spend one night in the hospital before heading home for the remainder of my recovery.

Three

Leaving Home

Once in life a gift is shown,
Make still the walk,
Stand straight the fence.
A word will tell,
The thought behind,
With spirit quenched,
A soul will find.

vfm

Isaac makes contact on a good pitch. The ball carries deep into the outfield. He begins his trot around the bases—a trot that will not bring him back to us for another time at bat.

I got to know Isaac when I coached my son's 8-10 year old Little League baseball team. Isaac was a frail kid—often taking time to rest after running the bases or after chasing down a fly ball. A heart problem limited his effort but not his desire and love for the game. All the simple things were exciting …. Wearing the uniform, walking to the plate, using a new glove, and being with the other players. It was never about winning. It seemed that it was always about the sensory pieces of the game. The taste of sunflower seeds being chewed in the dugout …. the smell of a new baseball …. the sound of a ball hitting a bat …. the sight of a proud parent watching their child reach the next base. Isaac reminded us of how Little League baseball was meant to be. He reminded us that somewhere along the way the game got pulled from his grasp. People stopped hearing what it really means to be children.

Some years after Isaac left us, his father sent this note to a group of Little League baseball coaches and parents—thanking them for the way they coached one of Isaac's younger brothers.

"**Subject:** Thanks for a great season!
From: Ben Harris
To: Henry Kitner, Zach Smith, Everett James
Sent: June 2008

I just wanted to pass along my thanks for a great season. I think you guys exemplify the spirit of our Little League 'Instructional Division'. I have had my kids in Little League for more than 15 years now, starting with my eldest daughter who is now in college. I have three children now in the League, and as some of you know, lost a son who also played in our Little League. He passed away the summer shortly after his 10th birthday in 2001 due to a heart condition that he had since birth. What I reflect on this year, I thought I should share for all concerned, as it really exemplifies the style I have seen over these past 15 years, and hope to see continue in our Little League.

First our story. It was the summer of 2000 and my son Isaac was 9. Coach Vic Mazzio had Isaac on his team for the third season and understood the limitations with his health. On May 2nd (Isaac's birthday), with similar rules that our Little League practices today, Isaac got his first opportunity to pitch. The inning before he was scheduled to pitch, Isaac was hit in the mouth with a baseball while playing second base. In dramatic fashion, dad had to carry him off the field to tend to his minor wound. I still have a picture of him nursing his mouth with ice while sitting next to his Grand-Dad. Coach Vic saw something of the moment and decided to try and have Isaac pitch as scheduled. He got down on one knee and said to Isaac, "I really need you to pitch next inning buddy …. Do you think you can do it for me?" Isaac didn't say anything, but nodded his head. The only inning Isaac ever pitched …. He struck out the first batter, second batter pop fly to the pitcher, third out routine ground ball to the pitcher and Isaac threw the boy out. On his very next at bat, the boys were chanting his name as he clipped a ground ball for a base hit and knocked in two runs. We won that day. The following season would be Isaac's last. He could no longer keep up with the fast balls and was limited in getting as far as first base. I don't believe the entire season he mustered a hit. Years after his passing, I still get to tell this story and sift through the Little League memorabilia we saved.

So to the point. I saw you guys work the practice this year of playing everyone equally, and at times, felt your self-doubt. The skill level of our team had dropped from previous years with some new players, and it was difficult to balance keeping the good players interested while giving everyone an opportunity. In my opinion, you guys struck the perfect cord. There are plenty of travel leagues for those parents that want hard competition. Our Little League spirit has always been to instruct all kids and to grow them equally. Congratulations on a successful season, and thanks again.

Happy Father's Day to All!!

Ben Harris"

> *Moment made by elder leading,*
> *Receive thy message—subtle given.*
> *Tale expressed from mind of borrow,*
> *Hear his soul—he now is teaching.*
>
> vfm

Young Isaac Harris taught me everything I needed to know about life inside the 'cancer locker room'. He taught me in the three years that we all played baseball with him that the best life is one free of competition …. the best life is one where nobody is excluded …. the best life is one where we are not judging …. the best life is one where comparison is absent. Isaac underwent his third heart surgery at the age of 10—just one month after we finished our 2001 Little League season. He passed shortly after that surgery and life for us was not the same for a very long time.

I was getting ready for my cancer surgery. Thinking about little Isaac gave me a special kind of strength. Thinking about my wife and children gave me all the strength I needed for this part of my cancer journey.

The 4 weeks between meeting my neck surgeon for the first time and my surgery day went by very quickly. The day arrived and I traveled with my wife to the 'premier' cancer institute where I would have my surgery. I took a little over 2 weeks off from work to have my cancer surgery and to recover from it. Surgery day was Friday, November 12, 2010.

The drive seemed rather long but it was only 60 minutes from our front door to the 'premier' cancer institute. We got there right around 10am—the time given to us by the staff that communicates the details of surgeries to the patient. I was due to go into surgery somewhere between 12 noon and 1pm in the afternoon. I was directed to go to a patient registration area of the hospital upon arriving at the hospital. We spent about 15-30 minutes with registration procedures before being taken up to the 'pre-op' waiting area where I got gowned and prepped for surgery. This area looked very much like an emergency room where each patient waiting to go into surgery had a hospital bed with a privacy curtain drawn around it. IV's were placed in my arms and I received my first visit from one of the two anesthesiologists that would be with me during my surgery. The second anesthesiologist visited with me shortly after the first one had left. They both wanted to make sure that I hadn't eaten anything within about 10 hours of arriving at the hospital. They also let me know that a breathing tube would be inserted into my esophagus shortly after I was put to sleep and it would be removed before I was due to wake-up in recovery. For a short period of time things were quiet. Me and my wife had time to be with each other—just the two of us. We didn't talk much about the surgery that was before us. At that moment I could hear myself reflecting on our beautiful married life together.

I wasn't scared to have the surgery. I was really excited and relieved to be this close to having the tumor removed from my neck and to begin living my life with a lesser amount of cancer talk around me. I remember feeling optimistic about the possibility of having an amazing surgery .... one that would prove to be a miracle by many measures .... one that would raise up this cancer patient with supposed insurmountable odds to a place of perfect joy. I believed in my oncologist and neck surgeon with an unconditional trust and gave them complete control of my life. My wife has always been the spine in our back .... the strong and steady one in uncertain times. Never giving consideration to thoughts of failure. She was no different in this moment—very confident that everything was going to work out for us.

My neck surgeon came to visit about 30 minutes before I was 'wheeled' into the operating room. He began marking the tumor site on my neck. The thing that I remember most about the 'grease pencil' marks that he made on my neck was the one that he made directly behind my right ear. This mark extended well above my ear and next to the mark he penciled his initials. Even though it is probably something that most—if not all—surgeons do before a surgery, for some odd reason it made me feel very calm and very accepting. At this moment, my life was in his hands. I put all of my trust in the work that he was about to do. He asked me how I was doing and how I was feeling. I told him that I felt very ready to have the surgery and that I was ready to move on to a life without cancer. He smiled his big smile and told me that all the right people would be in the room to make that happen. He said that he would see me in the operating room.

I was 'wheeled' into the operating room and lifted from the gurney to the operating table. Many people were already in the room—arranging surgical instruments, connecting me to monitoring equipment, and placing compression sleeves around my legs. As others entered the room, they came to the table and introduced themselves. The anesthesiologists took their place behind me and in a short while I fell asleep.

*Health of spirit,
Hope of heart,
Mend created,
Daily strengthen.*

vfm

I started to wake up from surgery in the recovery room as tubes and wires were being removed from my body. In just minutes, I was on my way to my hospital room. I was 'wheeled' into my hospital room where I would spend the night. I had drainage tubes in my neck and an incision that ran from the base of my neck—just below my chin—to about one inch above and behind my right ear. The total length of the incision was about 13 inches. I was on the operating room table for just over 8 hours. Thirty-nine (39) lymph nodes were removed from my neck—roughly 19 lymph nodes above the one lymph node that contained the tumor and 19 lymph nodes below the one lymph node that contained the tumor. Of those 39 lymph nodes, only the one containing the tumor was found to be cancerous. My surgery was done on a Friday. If all went well through the night, I would be able to leave the hospital and go home the very next day.

All through the night, nurses were in and out of the room caring for me. I remember seeing my roommate eating and I asked the nurse if there was a chance that I could get something to eat. She immediately got me a turkey sandwich and assured me that if I finished the entire sandwich, I would be taken off morphine and placed on Percocet. I ate the entire sandwich and 2 hours later—4 hours after the last injection of morphine into my IV—I was put on Percocet. I was really happy about this change. I hated the way the morphine was making me feel. It was getting close to 6am on Saturday morning—November 13, 2010—and I still hadn't slept for a nice long stretch of 4 hours or more. I was taking intermittent 'quick naps' that were lasting anywhere from 30-60 minutes at a time. Somehow this was enough rest for me. I wasn't feeling tired at all.

Two residents came in to visit with me at 7am. They were currently doing their residencies with my surgeon and both of them helped with my surgery. The more people that I started to talk with about my surgery the more I discovered that there were a lot of doctors, nurses, and medical staff in the operating room during my surgery. The residents checked my drainage tubes and removed the two that were in the back of my neck. I still had one drainage tube inserted at the base of my neck just below my chin. I was told that this tube would remain inserted for another week. I asked the two residents where my surgeon was and they said that he left shortly after my surgery to spend a weekend in the mountains. He picked a beautiful day for a break in the mountains.

Through the window of our room, I could see the sun rising up and the sky was clear. I asked the residents if I would be going home today and they said that my surgeon would let them know after they saw how my morning was going. They wanted me to get out of bed and start walking around the hallways. Just after they left, the nurse came in to see me and I had her help me out of bed so that I could start walking. She arranged all of my tubes so that they would hang from the little 'walking stand' that would accompany me on every walk. I also used this stand as my walking pole. It kept me from falling when I got dizzy during my walks.

My first walk around our hospital wing lasted about 10 minutes. I returned to my room to the sweet sounds of Luther Vandross. My roommate had a large portable stereo system and he was playing his tapes of Luther— 'old school' stereo system all the way. I sat down on my bed and just listened for a while. It was the right time to hear Luther Vandross singing his mellow songs. He went into the bathroom and at exactly that time the nurse who was just starting her shift came into our room. She introduced herself as Aimee and the first thing she said was I hate that music that Lawrence plays. He plays it all the time and I switch it to classical when he is in the bathroom. She went over to his stereo 'boom box' and switched to a classical music radio station. I said, "I'm okay with Luther Vandross …. and I'm guessing that Lawrence is not going to like that". She smiled and asked if I needed anything. I told her that I was 'good for now' and she left the room. Lawrence came out of the bathroom, heard the classical music playing on his 'boom box', and said, "I guess Aimee stopped in here". I said, "as a matter of fact …. yes …. she did". He chuckled through a smile and said, "For some reason she just doesn't like my Luther Vandross selections". He turned off his stereo system completely and for a few minutes we sat in silence. I told him my name was Vic and he told me his name was Lawrence but I could call him 'L' or 'La-Ro'. The 'La-Ro' came from the first two letters of his first name—Lawrence—and the first two letters of his last name—Roberts. I told him that I would use 'L' or 'La' if that was okay with him. He seemed to like 'La'— my one syllable shortened version of 'La-Ro'—so I called him 'La' most of the time and 'L' some of the time. He shortened my name to 'V' and I fully approved …. thinking that it was something cool.

'La' was in the hospital for a third go-around with cancer. The first was ten years ago and the second was 4 years ago. Each time the same cancer returned but in different areas of his body. His cancer was aggressively metastasizing and taking over more of his organs each time it returned. During our conversation his wife called and asked how he was doing. He broke down during the phone call while sitting right next to me. He kept saying to her, "I am so tired of fighting cancer …. I am really so tired. I can't fight anymore. I really just want to leave the hospital and come home to be with you". After a bit more conversation, he hung up the phone. He told me that his home is in Cincinnati, Ohio. He came to this 'premier' cancer institute to get the best cancer care in the country. He had been in the hospital for one week before I came into his room. His doctors were trying to build up his energy so that they could perform surgical procedures on his lungs and let him have a little break before starting chemotherapy treatments. This time around the cancer had spread to his lungs. He had cancer nodules in his lungs that were much bigger than the ones that I had in my lungs. He was in a serious fight for his life.

'La' went on my next walk with me. He said, "Hey 'V', I want to show you something …. follow me". He was getting around much better than me but he waited for me as we walked around the hallway loop. About halfway through our walk, he hurried ahead of me as we neared an area that was directly behind the nurses' station. He called back to me, "Hey 'V' …. Hurry up …. Come see this". I tried to move to where he was as quick as I possibly could. When I got there he had the door to a food pantry cabinet opened, the door to a refrigerator opened, and the door to a freezer opened. "Look at this", he said. "Free food anytime we want it". I was thinking that this was a jackpot. I said to him, "we can't just go into here without letting anyone know we're taking things". He said, "they are letting me get into the pantry, refrigerator, and freezer whenever I like because I will be here a long time and they want me to build up my energy …. Relax 'V' …. Just relax". Just then a nurse walked by and I asked her, "Lawrence is allowed to get food whenever he wants but am I?" She said, "Of course!" I looked at 'La' with the nurse still there and said, "Well, bro …. Game on!" All three of us laughed pretty hard. 'La' and I grabbed some gelatin cups, some crackers, and some soda before heading back to the room. When we finally got back to the room, I rested for about 15 minutes before eating the gelatin and drinking some of the soda. 'La' started playing his Luther Vandross music again—this time a little louder than before. He also had Marvin Gaye tapes which really got our little hospital party moving. Marvin Gaye singing 'Mercy Mercy Me', 'Ain't No Mountain High Enough', and 'I Heard It Through the Grapevine'. We had some completely amazing sounds coming from our room. I bet the neighbors were jealous. I thanked 'La' for his music. It was music that I listened to every once in a while and I enjoyed listening to it with 'La' by my side. I asked him to go back to Luther Vandross and play 'Having a Party'. We sat there listening to his music while we finished our snacks.

It was getting close to 11am and the two residents returned to visit with me. They checked my one remaining drainage tube to make sure it was collecting fluid properly. They also measured the amount of fluid that was in the little plastic 'catch flask' at the end of the drainage tube. The amount of drained fluid that they measured seemed to be right where they wanted it to be. One of the two residents left for about 15 minutes while the other resident continued to examine me and talk to me about how I was feeling, if I was eating, and if I had gotten out of bed to walk. I let him know that I was doing all of those things and he seemed very happy about it. The other resident returned to my room and let me know that he just finished having a phone conversation with my surgeon. They all thought that I was recovering nicely so I would be going home as soon as my wife could come to get me. Before leaving, the residents started to show me how I would need to clean my drainage tube at least a couple of times a day. They also let me know that visiting nurses would be coming to my house to check on me every day for the first week that I was home. They told me that the nurses would be helping me with everything else that I needed to know and do before I left the hospital. I thanked them for taking great care of me both during surgery and as I recovered in the hospital. We said good-bye to each other and then they left. I immediately called my wife and let her know that I was being released from the hospital and that she could come with the children to pick me up. She let me know that she would be at the hospital in about two hours.

I looked over at 'La' after all of my visits and hospital departure arrangements were finished. I said to him,

"Hey 'La' …. I'm going to get ready to leave." He replied, "I know 'V' …. I heard from all of the conversations. I thought—and was hoping—that you would be with me for at least a couple of days". I replied, "Get up …. Let's take a walk and get some snacks. Then we'll come back and listen to some Luther and Marvin". He smiled and came over to help me get out of my bed. We made the slow walk to the pantry and stayed there talking. I decided that I needed something cold and sugary like ice cream so I looked in the freezer and there were little popsicles. I grabbed a few of the grape ones— my absolute favorites—along with a small package of shortbread cookies from the pantry. 'La' grabbed some peanut butter crackers and a soda. We headed back to our room and 'La' put on another tape of Marvin Gaye that he had—songs by Marvin that we hadn't yet listened to. We did listen to 'Mercy Mercy Me' one more time and when I heard it this second time I was reminded that Robert Palmer does a version of it that he may want to listen to sometime. These times with 'La' were getting to be fun. We became really close in a very short period of time.

After me and 'La' finished our snacks, I went into the bathroom and tried to get cleaned up for my trip home. The nurse helped me with getting ready to take a quick pass under the shower. She set everything out for me and recommended some things I could try to keep my incision dry and my drainage tube dry during my shower. She left and told me to pull the alarm string if I ran into problems. I removed my hospital gown and took my quick pass under the shower. I was able to get dressed on my own—noticing along the way that I could hardly lift my right arm away from my waist. I also noticed that I had very little feeling along the right side of my neck where the incision was made. I got myself completely dressed in the bathroom and as I was about to re-enter our room—from the bathroom, I heard 'La' on the phone arguing with someone. I stepped back into our room from the bathroom. I gathered up my things and sat in the chair next to my bed and watched some television while 'La' continued on the phone. He came to me with his phone and asked for help with the insurance company. He whispered to me that he was confused about what they needed from him. I whispered back to him to relax. I told him, "We got this 'La', no problem". He gave me the phone and I spoke to the insurance person who was on the other end of the call. Together 'La' and I figured out what needed to be done with his insurance. It was a few simple things with policy numbers and claims—information that was tucked away on a few of the many pages he had in a folder. After we hung up the phone, we sat there talking until my wife and children came. He said I was lucky to have so many caring people around me who were only two steps away if I needed them. 'La' made the trip to this 'premier' cancer institute—from Cincinnati—with his wife by his side. She got him settled in then had to return to their home because she had to work. They really needed a steady income—especially at a time like this. She would come for a longer visit when his lung surgery got scheduled and his chemotherapy started. I told 'La' that he inspired me, and encouraged me and I was very thankful for that. I also told him that he gave me an amazing amount of ***hope***—that one important thing that every cancer patient needs more than anything else. I actually told him that I loved him for taking an interest in me and for making the early stages of my recovery enjoyable. I will truly miss Lawrence the most out of all the cancer patients that I met while I was inside the 'cancer locker room'.

I was returning home one day following my surgery—Saturday, November 13, 2010. My wife and children appeared in the doorway of our hospital room and I immediately introduced them to Lawrence. He smiled to them from his bed. As we left our room, I looked back at him and he smiled back at me. I listen to Luther Vandross and Marvin Gaye when I want to remember the special time that Lawrence and I shared at the hospital. I need this reminder from time to time because it puts my mind in the right place. It keeps my focus on figuring out ways to care for everyone. It reinforces the things that Lawrence taught me about never competing or comparing when it comes to the things of everyday life. I pray that he won his cancer battle and that he listens to Luther Vandross with his lovely wife—maybe thinking about me every once in a while.

In this retreat come clear one path,
Become this friend,
Through trouble pass.
Relentless seem,
Each day to walk,
Shall hear in piece,
To carry on.

vfm

I sat in the back of our van for the 1-hour drive home. I needed help getting into the van and I would certainly need help getting out of the van. We pulled into our driveway and started the process of getting me into the house. Lots of small steps and lots of stops along the way. I stayed in our ground floor family room for most of my first week. I had a vest pocket on some of my long sleeve flannel shirts that I used to hold the 'drainage flask'. Each day I tried to go up the stairs one step at a time—pausing on each step as I made my way to the top. After about an hour or two, I would come back downstairs—one step at a time—until I made it down one flight of stairs to the first floor.

My younger brother Justin—with whom I shared a bedroom when I was growing up—surprised me with a visit in the afternoon on this first day back home. He arrived late in the evening and planned to stay a couple of days. I was doing a lot of sleeping most of the time during that first week home but he and I stayed up from about 6pm in the evening of this first day home to about 4am on Sunday morning just talking. It was like growing up all over again. We talked about everything and anything just like when we were kids.

Late in the afternoon on Sunday, November 14, 2010, my other brother Garrett and my sister Melanie visited with their families. Garrett came into the family room where I was lying on the couch resting. I think the first thing he saw was my drainage tube and the bandage that covered my incision. I think the sight of that made him cry. Through his tears he said to me, "I love you, man". I smiled back at him and told him that he shouldn't worry—I was going to be okay. I told him that I loved him and thanked him for coming. We talked for a minute before he headed back into the kitchen to be with the rest of the family.

Almost everyone was gathering at our house for dinner which was made by Garrett's wife. A small group came to our house after they finished celebrating my mom's birthday at a nearby local restaurant—about 35 people in our house. By the time my mom got to our house it was about 6pm on Sunday evening. I made my way to our upstairs bedroom to get some better rest. I was standing next to our bed with my wife and daughter Kara in the room. I felt myself starting to 'black out' so I slid down the side of the bed and sat on the floor. I softly said to my wife, "I think I am fainting". My wife got in my face and yelled, "Victor …. Get up!! …. Wake up!!" Her voice sounded real distant and I heard a loud bang in my ear. It was the strong clap of her hands to keep me awake. It worked. Before completely 'blacking out', I slowly started to wake back up.

I remained on the bed in our room and people came up to visit with me. They all seemed surprised by the drainage tube in my neck and the incision dressing on my neck. Maybe the shocking part about the drainage tube was the bloody solution that was collecting in the drainage tube 'catch flask'. It looked disgusting but I was getting used to seeing it. The whole evening was nice for me. I got to spend a little bit of time with nephews, nieces, brothers, and a sister that I don't get to see every day.

On Monday, November 15, 2010, I received my first visit from the visiting nurse that was sent to me by the 'premier' cancer institute. She came at about 9am in the morning and spent close to two hours with me. I was glad that she came to check on me but I also wanted her to leave before she found anything seriously wrong with me. I know that probably sounds strange because normally you want these people to see the problems that you might be having when you have them. She checked all of my vital signs and sat with me for quite a while just to learn how I was feeling—where my head was with all the changes that were going on in my life. I remember asking her if there were any foods that I shouldn't be eating this early after my surgery and she said that I went through a lot so I should feel comfortable eating anything that I liked. I asked if I could have a nice piece of chocolate cake and she said "certainly …. and if you want, put a nice big scoop of ice cream on top of it." This was my kind of visiting nurse. She really helped me feel good about my recovery. She was scheduled to visit three times per week so I was scheduled to see her again on Wednesday, November 17, 2010—just two days from my first visit with her.

I continued seeing the visiting nurse as she made her visits and I became increasingly obsessed with having my drainage tube removed. My wife helped me clean the tube 2 times each day. I dreaded each and every cleaning. It involved thoroughly wiping down the tube with isopropyl alcohol, measuring the amount of fluid that collected in the small 'catch flask', emptying the small 'catch flask', and cleaning the 'catch flask'. Each time this process was done, I would have the most extreme headache in the front and right side of my head. After the first couple of cleanings, I noticed that it only took about 25 minutes for the headache to subside. In subsequent cleanings I knew that I only had to deal with the pain for about 25 minutes so I held my head in my hands and kept an eye on my watch. By the second day, I had my mind trained to wait for 25 minutes before getting concerned.

At the end of my first week after surgery, I went to see the surgeon and he was very pleased with my recovery. He pleasantly surprised me by removing the drainage tube from my neck. The amount of fluid draining from my neck had gone well below 25 milliliters which was an indication that the tube could be removed. This was a happy day. He scheduled me for another set of head and neck MRI scans both with and without contrast. I would have the scans recorded when we returned home after our usual Thanksgiving Day gathering at the house of my wife's aunt in New England. My oncologist ordered a PET/CT scan which would also be done when we returned home after Thanksgiving. This PET/CT scan would be done with FDG contrast as usual.

On knee to bend,
With wing appear,
For river wash,
To better heal.

vfm

I was never completely sure that I would be able to make the 6-hour drive to New England to celebrate Thanksgiving with my wife's family. We loaded up our van and left early on Wednesday morning—the day before Thanksgiving. I was looking forward to being with all of her family. Those times have always been fun for me, my wife, and our 3 children. The days are filled with a lot of tradition. Having certain appetizers. Having the large turkey surgically carved by big Uncle Mark. Having Uncle Mark make the best stuffing ever by using 3-4 sticks of butter. Having glorious mashed potatoes—my personal favorite …. and having my father-in-law offer an amazing Thanksgiving prayer. Seeing all of the aunts, uncles, and cousins on my wife's side of our family was always something that we look forward to because we don't get to see them very often.

We took many stops along the way but we made it safely to Aunt Allie's New England home where we would celebrate Thanksgiving. The drive was just over 6 hours. Many in the family were already there and they came out of the house to greet us as we pulled into the driveway. Big Uncle Mark gave me a firm handshake and a big smile as he always does and I was so happy to see him and everyone else. Joshua—the husband of my wife's cousin—is always happy to see all of us. He is much taller than the rest of us but is a lot like Uncle Mark. He gives big hugs and playful tackles in the snowy yard. He must have heard that I was sick so he greeted me with his big smile and a cautious gentle hug—no tackle in the grass. In some ways, I missed his tackles in the grass but on this particular trip I was happy that he greeted me in a concerned way. Everyone in my wife's family is an interesting character with amazing stories to tell and a genuine curiosity about how everyone is getting along.

We went to check-in at the hotel where we usually stay and then returned to Aunt Allie's house to help with Thanksgiving meal preparations. For brief moments, some of us broke away to play basketball and pick up odds and ends for the meal. Other family members were arriving throughout the day so we took time to greet them and visit with them for a while.

Thanksgiving morning was cold and sunny but everyone was squeezing in their exercise for the day by walking or running along the canal path. Running on the canal path was my Thanksgiving morning ritual in prior years but this year my condition limited me to short slow walks for exercise. My wife took a long walk with her cousin and her brother's wife as she usually does when we are visiting Aunt Allie for Thanksgiving. After she returned to the hotel, we went out with her father for my short slow walk. We walked over the large bridge that crossed the canal and paused several times to watch the water drop down over the falls leading into the town village. For all the times that we went to Aunt Allie's for Thanksgiving, we never walked the bridge and stopped to marvel at the falls.

It was beautiful—watching a subtle mist rise above the power filled falls. We went up to Aunt Allie's house after our exercising and Thanksgiving meal preparations were in full swing. For the rest of the morning, I spent a lot of time sleeping on the recliner which was tucked away in a corner of a secluded parlor leading into Aunt Allie's family room. Every once in a while my wife—also named Allie—her father and her mother checked on me to make sure that I was fine. At around 12 noon, we headed back to the hotel to get dressed for the afternoon meal.

Our Thanksgiving meal started right around 3pm. Allie's father gathered all of us around the main table and gave his amazing speech and blessing. Adults sat at the large main table and the 'younger generation' sat at a smaller table across the way. Everything was delicious as always. The table conversation is hardly ever serious at our Thanksgiving Day meal and that is really the way we like it. We tell stories and reminisce about funny and odd moments that we share while on vacations—helping us to really enjoy and appreciate the close bonds that we have with each other. Clean-up from the meal started around 5pm and everyone seemed to participate in some way. From the short and simple tasks of taking plates, utensils, and glasses to the sink for washing to the longer tasks of washing everything, drying everything, and returning everything to cupboards. After clean-up was finished, we relaxed in the parlor and family room. Some watched the football game on television while others continued 'catching-up'. Just being up and around for long periods of time was tiring for me during my recovery from surgery so I sat once again in the recliner and slept for a short while.

On Friday we started the day with some walking on the canal path. Everyone seemed to have individual plans for things that they wanted to do or places that they wanted to see. In the afternoon, we decided that we would take a tour of a local brew house. Some were interested in the beer tastings while others were seriously interested in how certain types of beer were made. I was more interested in being where everyone else was. I was enjoying being around everyone and watching the fun they were having. We traveled to the brew house and unloaded the cars. We toured the brew house in groups and got back together in a large tasting area of the brewery where we enjoyed a beer or two before heading back to Aunt Allie's house. I think one of my silly fond memories of our tour would be the foul smell. It wasn't pervasive but it was noticeable to my sensitive nose. I'm almost certain that it came from the bacterial reactions that occur during the brewing of the beer. My biggest memory would be how sensitive skilled people become to the subtle taste differences that separate one beer from another.

The tradition on the Friday night after Thanksgiving at Aunt Allie's is to enjoy a fish fry dinner at a popular local restaurant. The restaurant is within comfortable walking distance from Aunt Allie's beautiful home. Her house is decorated for Christmas with simple candle lights in all of the front windows and a wreath on the front door— very inviting. It's a little cold outside and the fresh snowfall is a pure palette for the large, all glass conservatory across the street. Colored lights from within the conservatory cast their brilliant colors onto fresh pure snow that has been falling since early this morning. The walk to the restaurant was not bad for me. It took longer than it normally does but along the way we passed by homes that showed their beauty in an unselfish way. We entered the restaurant and sat for a bit in a quaint bar area before being called into the main part of the restaurant. Many of us ordered the fish fry which—on this day—is the highlight item on the menu. Most of the children enjoy some of the other offerings on the menu which they find more appealing than the breaded or baked fish. We are never starved for great conversations and great stories at this meal. There is still so much to talk about and we spend a good portion of this evening hearing about new adventures that happened throughout this past year. The people in the restaurant and the atmosphere in the restaurant remind me of what life is like in a small New England town. Everyone seems to know everyone else but they are very accepting of newcomers to the neighborhood. This Friday night meal is always a big highlight for me when we come to Aunt Allie's for Thanksgiving because we don't have this sort of thing back where we live.

Mid-morning on Saturday, we packed up the van, checked out of the hotel, and drove up to Aunt Allie's to say our 'good-byes' to everyone. Most had already left by the time we got there but the few that remained are like us …. they don't want this tradition filled Thanksgiving weekend to end. We left hesitantly to resume our busy lives in nearby busy places …. looking forward to gathering again at Aunt Allie's in a couple of years.

The PET/CT scan that was ordered by my oncologist before Thanksgiving was completed on that first Monday after returning home from Thanksgiving. I met with my oncologist to review the results on Wednesday morning of that same week. He said that I was getting around well. The scans showed no signs of cancer in my neck area. The nodules in both lungs were still appearing vividly on scans—presenting as cancerous regions with FDG contrast injected. For the time being, we were going to continue watching these nodules—closely following any change in the number of them and in the size of them. We were still considering immunotherapy but we were going to wait for a bit to make decisions around that while carefully monitoring my lung situation with PET/CT scanning every three months for the next 3-5 years. I was not a candidate for some of the gene specific melanoma therapies that were currently available to patients in clinical studies. My oncologist also thought that at this point there would be more risk than reward with chemotherapy or radiation therapy approaches for my head and neck or for the nodules that were being detected in my lungs. I would see him again in 3 months when I was scheduled to have my next PET/CT scan.

MRI scans were completed one week after the PET/CT scans—just about 3 weeks after my 'right neck dissection' surgery. I met with my head and neck surgeon on Thursday afternoon of that same week to review the MR imaging results. My neck surgeon was excited to see no signs of cancer in tissue regions surrounding the 39 lymph nodes that were excised. He explained that melanoma was found in just the lymph node where the large tumor growth was located. The entire tumor growth was melanoma. Cancer cells were not detected in any of the other 38 lymph nodes that were removed during surgery. He was very excited about this finding as well. He said that I should schedule physical therapy to help restore full movement in my right shoulder and arm. He also said that some of the feeling on the right side of my neck would return over time but certainly not all of it. The surgery was extensive and nerves in that area were effected as part of the dissection. He also asked about other therapies that I would be having and thought that—at the very least—immunotherapy should be considered in an adjuvant therapeutic context. Similar to the future appointments scheduled with my oncologist, I would be visiting with him every 3 months for the next 2-3 years.

Four

Tree Forts and Go-Carts

Air supports,
Foot to treadle,
Growth expected,
Slim to wander.

vfm

I tend to believe that each of us needs a home and a way to get there. We need a safe place to explore what we're about and to be who we really are. Our own little space in the world that is free of judgment and ridicule with a path leading us to it. At the age of 8, I guess I thought that a tree fort was home and a go-cart was the way to get there. And so, I began to build and explore.

The 'tree fort industry' was booming in the sixties. For that matter, so was the 'go-cart industry'. In my neighborhood alone there were five kids with a tree fort AND a go-cart. I felt lucky to be one of them. My engineering, materials acquisition, and assembly staff was a close knit group of dedicated and competent individuals…..my brothers and my sister. Resources for building were plentiful as the homes in our neighborhood were still being built. The builder didn't mind if we helped ourselves to lumber and nails as long as it was 'scrap'.

Over time, our forts and go-carts became complex and our definition of 'scrap' changed. Uncut 8 foot lengths of 2x4 lumber were made to stretch beyond what seemed to be the limits of a safe tree fort. Frank Lloyd Wright called it cantilevering …. we called it 'floating'. Stretched out over the branches of a tree—seemingly unsupported—were our structures of freedom. These were vulnerable places for children to be. These were places without the loving guidance of a parent's hand.

From these floating wooden decks, we could see over the expansive cornfield that backed up to our yard. The rows of corn went on for years. Even though the farmer planted in the Spring and harvested around September, it all melted together when we were 'floating'. We couldn't tell when it started or when it ended. I don't think we ever cared.

There was always something to be done in the tree fort. Nails that were going to be re-used had to be straightened. Branches had to be trimmed. Tours for the curious had to be given. Significant pieces of each day were spent with no plan of where to begin or where to end …. refreshingly seamless. It all seemed to take care of itself …. much like the cornfield …. very much like home. All things working together without squeaking. No clock in sight. No record of how much got accomplished, how well things were done, or who did them. There existed a definite balance without record or want of record. I think home is all of these things. An intuitive place that we know thoroughly but have trouble finding sometimes. Home is found when we clear away the clutter of today and wait patiently. Home is found when we 'float'.

We worked on the tree fort every day. Sometimes adding to what was already in place and other times starting over with a set of fresh new ideas. At the beginning of one particular day, my father stood our construction team at the edge of the driveway and shared some of the tree fort 'building code' with us. He spoke as the group of us looked over the back yard in the direction of the tree fort. "Look at all of those beautiful trees at the edge of the yard. I want each of you to know that those are MY trees. I love them dearly and I particularly love the way they are right now. I would not like for anything more to be added to them. When I return from work at the end of the day, I want to stand in this same spot and see the exact same thing that I see right now …. Beautiful trees and one small tree fort". He left for work and we gathered together for a 'construction meeting'. All of us agreed that my father's interest was on the wellbeing of the trees. Based on the new 'building code' restrictions, it seemed perfectly reasonable to now build a small house that would rest on the ground just behind the woodpile. We began construction immediately.

As always, we shuttled wood through the cornfield from new home sites in our neighborhood to a spot behind the woodpile at the back edge of our yard. We knew exactly where to enter and exit by the shape and size of the trees that separated each of the neighborhood properties from the cornfield. By this time, we had developed a very efficient—and legal—materials acquisition process. Wood sorting, nail straightening, and general materials integrity inspection activities followed along very quickly. By 10am, we were into full construction without any kind of blueprint. Our 'sensory carpentry tools' seemed to guide the raising. It felt right to the touch as we slid our hands across the wood. It looked like it would fit our needs perfectly. The pleasing smell of fresh cut lumber kept hammer to nail.

Go carts travel along the path that leads home. The ride is filled with uncertainty, confusion, anticipation, excitement, and fear—elements that somehow manage to clear away the clutter of the world, grab hold of our deepest thoughts, and guide us home.

My brother would test the changes that we made on our go-cart as we prepared for a day of riding. So much went wrong before so little went right. He laid himself out there in true test pilot fashion without question. Strapping into a cart that seemed to have a mind of its' own. It became a daily wrestling of wits….us against a machine. Challenges and opportunities arose when we tried to start, stop, turn, or change speeds. We learned more during these moments than when we moved in a straight line at a constant speed. We soon realized that we were holding on to what we thought was a steering wheel and we were pressing our feet against what we thought was a brake.

Masking sense of life to shelter,
Smaller hand will grasp and offer.
Pass a year where growth is showing,
Now too small for future knowing.

vfm

Childhood is a funny experience. Trudging through its' lessons seems a rather slow and deliberate process. Items of knowledge are presented and taken in sequence so that a growing mind can absorb all that is needed for future journeys. Always time to reflect. The small hand of youth has time to grasp life …. turn it over and look at it from all sides …. understand it thoroughly. The adult hand seems to be too small for this same approach to understanding life.

Begin this tree a walk so long,
With hope to shade,
And help to grow.
A branch will reach one former step,
Renewing past,
To stretch beyond.

vfm

I returned from our Thanksgiving celebration at Aunt Allie's with a new set of thoughts …. an original set of thoughts. The canvas was clear and I felt like a child again. I remember feeling like my surgery cleared away some of the cluttered spaces in my mind. Being at Aunt Allie's for Thanksgiving tends to do that for me. It's like a reset in many ways. I take a closer look at all that I have accumulated in my mind and heart over the year and make decisions about what to keep and what to release. It is a natural and necessary process.

I continued to be surprised and excited as my walks became farther and faster and my arm and shoulder started to work like they used to. I was getting occasional questions about my health from people who heard about my cancer and I started to pray deeply at the chapel in our church. Sometimes I would go to chapel well before the start of services and sit by myself thinking that I might be 'that miracle' …. praying that I would be 'that miracle'. I gave myself to the care of my doctors, nurses, and my God. I gave them my full trust. I was looking to them for hope.

My life is not revolving around my cancer as much as it was before the surgery. I am getting favorable results from the PET/CT scans and the MRI scans. As long as this keeps happening, my mind will be free of concern for the three months that I have between scans. I now have more time to do some of the things with my wife and children that I have always wanted to do.

My youngest son Reid is playing baseball in high school and many nights during each week, we spend hours in the full size batting cage that we built at the end of our backyard. The cage has lights so that we can hit at night. We also have a pitching machine so that we can 'rep' on certain pitch locations within the strike zone. Baseball players love hitting off of live pitching but the real benefit from hitting off of a pitching machine revolves around this concept of doing large amounts of repetition on pitches in areas of the strike zone that are sometimes hard to hit. Going out to the cage to hit has been therapeutic for me during these weeks and months of recovery. The exercise of carrying a bucket of balls and a pitching machine out to the cage 4 nights a week to hit just under 200 pitches has been a nice measure of my returning fitness level. My son carries the equipment out to the cage and I just need to 'show up' so that I can feed the pitching machine. For part of our workout, I will sit on a ball bucket behind the 'L-screen' and toss baseballs to him from close range so that he can practice waiting on outside pitches and starting his swing a little sooner on inside pitches—really focusing on driving outside pitches to right field and driving inside pitches to left field. The work that we do is helping me get my shoulder and arm movements back in a controlled way. This is the sport that I grew up playing. It is the one thing that has been constant in my life. I am using it now to bring me back to the way I used to be.

It has been three months since my neck tumor surgery and I am heading to the 'premier' cancer institute for my PET/CT scan. As always, I will be having a scan with FDG contrast. The purpose of this scan is to see if my neck remains clear of cancer and to see if any new cancer sites have presented in other areas of my body. I sit down in the imaging suite and wait to be called back to one of the many imaging preparation rooms where I will be injected with the FDG contrast agent before having CT and PET scans recorded. After only 5 short minutes of waiting, a nurse called my name and invited me to walk back to the imaging area. Along the way, she asked me how I was doing with all that is going on with my cancer. I told her that I was in a good place with my thinking and that I believed in my doctors. I also told her that all through my illness I have been strengthened by my wife and 3 children. They just seem to know when to ask questions and when not to talk about my cancer. I love them for that. She introduced herself as Abby and told me that she has been married to the same wonderful husband for 30 years. They have 5 children who are grown up and doing well. She asked me how our Christmas went and I told her that everyone was home and we had an enjoyable 2-week vacation with each other. She went on to tell me that for the first time ever she knitted the sweater that she was wearing and gave it to herself as a Christmas present. I asked her if she went so far as to wrap it and she admitted that she did. I complimented her on how beautiful the sweater looked. She knitted the sweater in just 3 weeks. I told her that my wife Allie was taught how to knit and crochet by a friend of ours and she enjoyed doing it. Allie kept practicing her knitting until she was able to knit a few beautiful blankets that we use all the time. Abby admitted that she learned how to knit as a young girl. The skill was passed on to her by her mother. She stuck with it and took on bigger knitting 'projects' as the years passed and her skills got better. We arrived at the imaging preparation waiting room and Abby said that my family sounded strong and that they would carry me through my cancer journey. She gave me a hug and said that she would keep me in her prayers.

Getting a PET/CT scan was actually becoming a bit monotonous but it seemed to me like the single best way to quickly see if cancer therapies and surgeries were working. I went into the preparation room and received my FDG injection. Right after I received the injection, I needed to consume my 32 ounce 'radioactive cocktail'. This time I had about 20 minutes to drink all of it. After about 25 minutes, I was taken to the imaging room where my full body scan was recorded. From start to finish the scanning took about 50 minutes. I was directed out of the imaging area and allowed to go home.

Four days after my PET/CT images were recorded, I met

with my oncologist to review the findings. He said that everything was still about the same. My neck was not 'lighting up' so it was clear of cancer. No new cancer sites were seen on the scan but my lung nodules had increased in size a little bit. The number of them was the same but the size in several of them had increased. I was alarmed by this news but he said that we were still in a 'watch and wait' stage with the lung nodules. Overall it was a very good result. I called my wife and let her know that it was a 'cupcake day'. We came up with this idea to start celebrating good imaging results with a cupcake treat. We started calling a day of good imaging results a 'cupcake day'. My oncologist was happy to see that I was in such good spirits and—as to plan—he said that I would have my next PET/CT scan in 3 months.

One week later I went back to the 'premier' cancer institute to have MRI scans recorded on my head and neck. My neck surgeon ordered my scans to be recorded both without gadolinium contrast and with gadolinium contrast. I started scheduling my scans for early in the morning because I needed to fast in order to reach the desired blood sugar level of 96-98 milligrams per deciliter (mg/dL). It became easiest to achieve this blood sugar level if I ate a light dinner the night before the test and then traveled to the 'premier' cancer institute for imaging right after I woke up in the morning. Additionally, I would try to get just 4 hours of sleep the night before testing so that I could fall into a partial sleep while I was in the imager and the scans were being recorded. This was my very simple way of getting around any claustrophobia that might develop while I was in the imager.

Both MRI scans—with and without gadolinium contrast—were completed in about 60 minutes. Five days after MR imaging, I met with my neck surgeon and he let us know that it was a 'cupcake day'. Everything looked good in my head and neck. The tumor site remained clear of cancer and no new sites were present in my head or neck. As we had planned, my neck surgeon ordered my next MR imaging to be done in 3 months.

PET/CT and MRI scans were recorded in both May and August of 2011 as planned. Both months yielded 'cupcake day' results. My oncologist and neck surgeon were very encouraged by the absence of cancer sites in my scans. We were still keeping a watchful eye on the nodules in my lungs. So far the nodules hadn't really advanced noticeably in the imaging signatures that they presented. The next planned imaging was in November of 2011—one full year from the date of my cancer surgery and more than one year from my initial stage 4 cancer diagnosis.

Between my May 2011 and August 2011 imaging sessions, I got to do something that I wished I would have been able to do with my father. My older son Bryce was made the coach of Reid's Junior Legion summer baseball team …. and I was his assistant coach. I always wanted to coach baseball with my father but never got the chance to do so because my father became very sick at a young age. Now I had the chance to coach with one of my children.

Our season started with a game that took us into extra innings. We were the visiting team so each extra inning started with our team going ahead by one run and then the home team responding with a tying run in the bottom of the inning. This 'back and forth' lasted for 5 extra innings. We were running out of pitchers so we started to use position players that had strong arms and accurate throwing capabilities. Bryce coached us through this very tough challenge with our pitchers. With his guidance, we found our way through one more inning where we scored two runs in the top of the inning and the opposing team did not score a run in the bottom of the inning. That was one of our best wins of the season. Bryce was making lineups and substitutions and managing our pitching staff so that we could have healthy arms starting every game. We had a very competitive season that year and applied a novel defensive shift against a team that was stocked with talented players—many of whom would go on to play in DI college baseball programs. It was the first shift of infielders and outfielders that I had seen before the shifting of defensive players became popular. Bryce finished that season of coaching by helping to coach the

Western Conference team in our Junior Legion All Star game.

I received 'cupcake day' results in my November 2011 imaging tests and the doctors were encouraged. They both wanted to hit significant milestone marks for cancer remission—which come at 5 years and 10 years—before getting overly excited about me being cured of cancer. Things were progressing nicely. After being free of cancer for one year, my oncologist made the decision to not apply adjuvant immunotherapies, chemotherapies, or radiation therapies at this critical time. This decision would change if my condition changed for the worse at some point in the future.

Carpentry has always been one of my passions. From a very early age, I loved working with wood. More than any other medium, it is forgiving. You can bend it a little …. Not always make the sharpest cuts …. and make other little 'intentional mistakes' so that pieces of wood will fit together—all without ever compromising the mechanical integrity of the overall structure. Metal, glass, tile, and concrete are not forgiving. You must be accurate with your cuts and measurements. You can almost never force pieces to fit together without breaking, chipping, or creating cracks in the pieces. Maybe it was this forgiving nature of wood that drew me to it at a young age.

Our laundry room needed a re-design and a reconstruction. I was between cancer imaging so I had time to start the work that needed to be done to turn the laundry room into a utilitarian space. Many things needed to change in the current space. We needed to replace the original 2x4 framing with 2x6 framing so that we could increase the insulation thickness—especially on the outside walls. The door leading out to the garage needed to be moved so that it wouldn't interfere with the door leading out to the backyard. The entire space could be split into an adequately sized laundry area that is isolated from a welcoming entry area by a pocket door. In-floor heating under a new simulated wood ceramic tile floor would make the room cozy during the cold winter months. Finally, a fire proof door leading out to the garage would bring the space up to code and some masonry work would 'square up' the opening for a new thermal door leading out to the backyard.

It took a few months to build a raised wooden floor deck for the laundry room area of the space. The entry area would have the existing concrete slab as it's floor deck. Once this raised wooden deck was completed, new 2x6 walls were framed into the space. Two new 20 amp circuits were run from the breaker box that was located on the wall at the opposite end of the house. These circuits would be used to feed the recessed lights in the ceiling, the washing machine, and the outlets along the walls. A new dedicated circuit was also run for the dryer in the laundry area. The pocket door separating the laundry area from the entry/reception area was the perfect solution for space economy when it came to opening and closing doors. The new door to the garage opened toward the pocket door and was located at end of the entry/reception area closest to the laundry room. A new concrete lintel was built above the new thermal door leading to the backyard. Beautiful panel heaters—one in the laundry area and one in the entry/receiving area—were tied into the existing hot water baseboard heating system. In the new design, one end of the entry/reception area was open to the kitchen and the opposite end of the entry/reception area led into the laundry area through the pocket door. All of these parts of the renovation were completed within a 2-year time frame. The laundry space was useable within 3 weeks of starting the project. I continue to build interior features into both the laundry area and the entry/reception area. A large pantry cabinet was built along the wall that separates the garage from the entry/reception area. This cabinet is used as a pantry for the kitchen. The entire space is useable but lacks the design finishes that will make it look incredible. Hopefully we will get all of it completed before my 5-year 'cancer-free' milestone.

I received 'cupcake day' results again for my February 2012 imaging tests and the doctors were once again encouraged. We were sticking with the plan to image every 3 months for the first five years. During the collection of these February 2012 scans, I got to spend time in conversation with Katy as I waited in the PET/CT prep room and drank my 'radioactive cocktail'. Her story was very similar to mine except she had melanoma that hadn't yet reached a lymph node or internal organs. Her PET/CT results would be used to stage her cancer and see if any other cancer sites existed in her body. I was in her spot about a year and 3 months ago. I knew exactly what kind of thoughts were running through her mind. Her doctor and oncologist conversations weren't as discouraging as mine but she was really scared. She was 32 …. married to a pretty cool guy named Aaron and caring for her little 2-year old daughter Rachel. Aaron and Rachel didn't know what to think and Katy seemed overwhelmed—not sure what her next steps would be. I told her my story and she started to cry a little bit. I asked her why she was crying and she said that she didn't want that kind of misery to happen to her. I told her that it was easiest for me to live in the 'minutes'. I was feeling fine in this immediate minute and I prayed that I would feel fine in each and every 'next immediate minute' …. all the while, building strength, becoming more hopeful, and keeping my spirits high by celebrating the glory in each minute of life that God provided. I listened intently as she told her story. Everything about her cancer scared her immensely. She said that Aaron was strong and Rachel was too young to know …. but she didn't ever want to be taken away from Rachel's happy smiling face. Rachel was her everything.

Be now this time,
To speak of never,
With breathless quake,
I see forever.

vfm

I have been 'cancer free' for 9 years now. All of my scans through my 5-year milestone continued to be 'cupcake days'. By year three, I was able to release all of my fear and rest it in the hands of God. My amazing doctors told me that we picked a path and we stuck to it. All along the way we didn't lose hope in the path that we chose. They told me that I inspired them and I told them that I believed in them from the very first day that we met. They walked side-by-side with me as we made this uncertain journey …. their strong voice in my ear …. their firm hand on my heart.

Epilogue

I got to walk my daughter Kara down the aisle at her wedding when she was joined for life to Adam—her best friend. At the wedding reception I shared the following words with all that were gathered....

"I am going to offer a prayer but before I do, I would like to share some thoughts .... have a conversation with you about what today could possibly mean for each one of us.

Some of you may be familiar with Jimmy Valvano—a legendary coach in college basketball. In 1993, he was given an Arthur Ashe ESPY Courage Award primarily for his battle with cancer. In his acceptance speech, he admonished each of us to do three very important things each and every day. The first thing we should do each day is laugh. We should spend some time in laughter. The second thing we should do each day is think deeply—spend some portion of each day in deep thought .... and the third thing is to have our emotions moved to tears .... the kind of tears that come from deep inside .... tears from the heart. 'Jimmy V' promised us that a day with these three pieces will be a 'full day' .... a 'heckuva day' .... a BEST DAY.

All of us have something in common .... Something that we share. In some way, Kara and Adam have already given each of us this gift of a BEST DAY. At times they have made us laugh. At times they have made us think deeply

…. and at times they have brought our emotions to tears. Today we gather with them again …. looking for that gift of a BEST DAY. If we are open to laughing along with them …. thinking deeply with them …. and being tearful with them, today will easily be that BEST DAY that we seek.

Allie, Karyn, Patrick, and I welcome you to the wedding celebration of our children …. Kara and Adam. We are glad you are here to share in what we know will be one of the BEST DAYS of their life together.

Let us pray ….

Dear Lord ….

Bless Kara and Adam as they begin this walk together. In laughing moments, we ask that you be their source of happiness.

In thoughtful moments, we ask that you be their counsel …. And in sad tearful moments, we ask that you be their strength.

Shelter them when rain falls ….
Carry them when the path is not clear ….
Lift them high when the sun is shining brightly on their face.

For this wonderful day and for all who are making it possible, we thank You.

We will think of You often as we enjoy this BEST DAY that you provide to all gathered here in Your name.

AMEN"

I also got to be a part of the induction of my 1983 Riscyne High School baseball team into the High School Baseball Hall of Fame in 2017. Leading up to our induction, each member of the team had to submit a 'letter of nomination' to the Hall of Fame nomination committee. Here is the letter that I submitted ….

"Hall of Fame Nomination Committee,

In June of 1983, the Riscyne High School baseball team completed an undefeated season and won the state baseball championship. As with most famed teams and sports programs, on the day that we won that state championship, we received a 'voice' …. we became part of a bigger, more important conversation. We became part of a conversation involving groups of people that need inspiration. We became part of a conversation involving groups of people that need hope. We became part of a conversation involving groups of people that need to know that the impossible is truly possible.

At the time of our achievement, we did not know that along with our new 'voice' came a set of obligations and a set of responsibilities. Over the years following our incredible accomplishment, each member of our historic team—coaches, assistants, and players alike, used their inherited 'voice' to share our amazing baseball story and inspire people to do great things—beyond high school baseball, beyond men's sports, and beyond high school in general. This was—and continues to be—an amazing 1983 high school baseball story with a limitless reach that extends beyond state and societal boundaries. It is a reach that enables us to inspire others to pursue impossible tasks with an expectation that success will be achieved. It is this limitless reach that distinguishes our 1983 Riscyne High School baseball team from other high achieving high school baseball Hall of Fame nominees.

Time must go on before the far reaching impact of a famed accomplishment can be measured. Time has gone on and our impact continues to be felt by many people beyond the confines of Riscyne High School and beyond the confines of high school baseball. The inherited 'voice' of that celebrated 1983 team has been heard and continues to be heard. It is now time for our team to take their well-deserved place in the High School Baseball Hall of Fame—standing next to the distinguished chosen who have entered before us.

As players, assistants, and coaches on that 1983 baseball team, we each have stories to tell. Stories describing the way we felt in 1983 when we achieved our goals and stories of how we have used our inherited 'voice' to inspire others. Some of us have coached baseball at all levels, some of us have played baseball at the college level and at the professional level, and some of us have been involved with the administrative aspects of sports. Many of us have children that excel in sports with some excelling in baseball. Our involvement in these many and varied contexts has served to develop and extend our limitless reach to those groups of people that need to hear our inspirational story the most.

Our strength and well defined purpose came from our amazing head coach—Jim Richards. He holds a seat in the High School Baseball Hall of Fame and always lived his life with an interest in inspiring us and others to do great things. He will be remembered for his impact on high school baseball and for the gentle way he motivated people. I think in some special way we also draw strength from Zach Douglas—a captain on our 1983 team. Over time, he has become bigger than life—coaching and teaching at Riscyne High School and advancing the sport of baseball on a daily basis. Many look to him for inspiration and he always has it to share. He will be a "captain" to many people for a long time.

Shortly after our 1983 baseball season ended, I received a note from Jim Richards. Along with this note he sent a picture of me in my Riscyne baseball uniform. I came to understand some of the important aspects of his simple message after my very recent battle with Stage 4 cancer. This was an impossible situation with doctors talking to me about having 6 months to live and with other doctors talking to me about hospice care. Through the fog of cancer, I discovered that hope conquers fear—in all situations. In many ways, Jim Richards was not fearful of future baseball success at Riscyne because he was drawing hope from the success and promise of our amazing 1983 team. I hope that during your review of nominees for the 2017 High School Baseball Hall of Fame, you give weight to the impact that our team has on people that need hope, inspiration, and encouragement to 'take on' impossible tasks. If this is made a part of your discernment process, it is certain that our 1983 Riscyne Baseball Team will enter the High School Baseball Hall of Fame in 2017."

I love my wife. I love my children. I love and thank all of my heroes who brought me to the point of living cancer free for so many years now. I'm hoping that from some of my stories you have an idea of what life was like for me as I sat inside the 'cancer locker room'.

There are extreme amounts of love in this room and there is never any judgement. There is an endless reservoir of hope in this room and there is never any competition or comparison. The 'cancer locker room' is filled with the best of all people. You don't have to look very far to find this love when you are in this room.

In some ways, I think that cancer is a gift from God. Having cancer and being side-by-side with cancer patients is the key that opens the 'cancer locker room' door. A chosen many get their key to the real 'cancer locker room'. Of this group, only a select 'some' survive …. getting to leave the 'cancer locker room' and tell others that they might have just experienced a piece of God's heaven.

www.ingramcontent.com/pod-product-compliance
Lightning Source LLC
Chambersburg PA
CBHW071354080526
44587CB00017B/3107